A Contemporary Woman Embraces The Eternal Circle...

Since Lynn V. Andrews saw a beautiful American Indian marriage basket in a modern California art gallery and traced its origins to the ancient Sisterhood of the Shields, a group of shaman Northwest Indian women, she has committed herself to an odyssey of self-discovery and spiritual growth called the Medicine Way.

She has shared this intimate story of her soul-quest in a series of books that have tapped into our deepest desires to understand the very core of our being...to feel fulfillment and inner peace...and to control our fate. Now, in *Windhorse Woman*, Lynn Andrews reaches the ending of one phase of her development...and finds a new beginning.

With her mentor, Agnes Whistling Elk, and Ruby, another Northwest Indian woman, she travels to distant Nepal to experience an unexpected resolution of her most primal needs. For here, amid haunting images of desire, death, and rebirth, she will learn an essential lesson about love and unity...one that speaks through a woman's heart to forge our visions and our lives.

"A GLIMPSE OF OTHER REALITIES...WE'RE REMINDED ONCE AGAIN OF THE POWER OF OUR THOUGHTS AND THE CRIPPLING EFFECTS OF FEAR AND SELF-LIMITATION."
—*San Francisco Chronicle* on *Star Woman*

"SHE SPEAKS OF RECLAIMING HER PERSONAL POWERS AS A WOMAN...THROUGH A WEALTH OF PRACTICAL SHAMANISTIC LORE INTERWOVEN WITH TALES OF SORCERY. ANDREWS REVEALS BOTH THE CHALLENGE AND THE REWARDS OF THE SACRED QUEST."
—*New Dimensions* on *Jaguar Woman*

D0951673

WINDHORSE
WOMAN

❧ *A Marriage of Spirit* ❧

LYNN V. ANDREWS

WARNER BOOKS

A Time Warner Company

If you purchase this book without a cover you should be aware that
this book may have been stolen property and reported as "unsold
and destroyed" to the publisher. In such case neither the author nor
the publisher have received any payment for this "stripped book."

Also by Lynn V. Andrews

Star Woman
Crystal Woman

This is a true story.
Some of the names and places in this book
have been changed to protect the privacy of those included.

Copyright © 1989 by Lynn V. Andrews

Book Design by Nick Mazzella

Text illustrations by Fanny Zucchiatti

Cover illustration by Susan Seddon Boulet

Cover design by Wendell Minor

All rights reserved.

Warner Books, Inc., 666 Fifth Avenue, New York, NY 10103

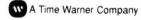 A Time Warner Company

Printed in the United States of America

First Trade Printing: September 1990

10 9 8 7 6 5 4 3 2

Library of Congress Cataloging-in-Publication Data

Andrews, Lynn V.
    Windhorse woman / Lynn V. Andrews.
        p.   cm.
    ISBN 0-446-39172-7
    1. Andrews, Lynn V.   2. Whistling Elk, Agnes.   3. Cree Indians—
Religion and mythology.   4. Shamans—Biography.   5. Chepang
(Nepalese people)—Religion   6. Shamanism—Tibet.   7. Shamanism—
Nepal.   I. Title.
E99.C88A55 1989
299'.7'092—dc20   89-40030
    [B]   CIP

For James Winfield Staples
who helped me understand
the Sacred Dream

I would like to acknowledge and thank my mother, Rosalyn Staples, for her caring and wonderful help, and Paul Talmage, Katherine Duckworth, Jack Crimmins, Al Lowman, Leslie Keenan, Padmavati, Cyrena Kopcha and Robert Shuster for their ceaseless energy and love.

Rumi, untitled poem, copyright © 1986 by Threshold Books, RD 3, Box 1350, Putney, Vermont 05346. Reprinted by permission of the publisher.

John Joseph Crimmins, from "Dreaming the Roads," copyright © 1989 by John Joseph Crimmins. Reprinted by permission of the author.

John Joseph Crimmins, from "Leaving," copyright © 1989 by John Joseph Crimmins. Reprinted by permission of the author.

John Joseph Crimmins, from "The Young Rider," copyright © 1989 by John Joseph Crimmins. Reprinted by permission of the author.

John Joseph Crimmins, untitled poem, in PRAYERS FOR THOSE WHO WILL NOT LEAVE THE CITIES, copyright © 1989 by John Joseph Crimmins. Reprinted by permission of the author.

John Joseph Crimmins, from "Body Music," copyright © 1989 by John Joseph Crimmins. Reprinted by permission of the author.

Elizabeth Herron, from "Reclamation," copyright © 1989 by Elizabeth Herron. Reprinted by permission of the author.

Elizabeth Herron, from "Leaving," copyright © 1989 by Elizabeth Herron. Reprinted by permission of the author.

Elizabeth Herron, from "Last Winter," copyright © 1989 by Elizabeth Herron. Reprinted by permission of the author.

John Joseph Crimmins, from "Grief," copyright © 1989 by John Joseph Crimmins. Reprinted by permission of the author.

Rumi, untitled poem, copyright © 1986 by Threshold Books, RD 3, Box 1350, Putney, Vermont 05346. Reprinted by permission of the publisher.

Elizabeth Herron, from "The Wild Weeds," copyright © 1989 by Elizabeth Herron. Reprinted by permission of the author.

Rumi, untitled poem, copyright © 1986 by Threshold Books, RD 3, Box 1350, Putney, Vermont, 05346. Reprinted by permission of the publisher.

John Joseph Crimmins, from "Hands," copyright © 1989 by John Joseph Crimmins. Reprinted by permission of the author.

Elizabeth Herron, from "Animal," copyright © 1987 by Elizabeth Herron. Reprinted by permission of the author.

John Joseph Crimmins, from "The Hollow Mind," in BLIND CORNERS, Paper Boats Press, Los Angeles, CA. Copyright © 1989 by John Joseph Crimmins. Reprinted by permission of the author.

Rumi, untitled poem, copyright © 1989 by Threshold Books, RD 3, Box 1350, Putney, Vermont 05346. Reprinted by permission of the publisher.

Jack Gilbert, from "Islands and Figs," copyright © 1982 by Jack Gilbert. Reprinted from MONOLITHOS by Jack Gilbert, by permission of Alfred A. Knopf, Inc.

Philip Lamantia, from "Horse Angel," in THE BLOOD OF THE AIR, copyright © 1970 by Philip Lamantia. Reprinted by permission of the author.

John Joseph Crimmins, from "Entering the Unknown," in BLIND CORNERS, Paper Boats Press, Los Angeles, CA. Copyright © 1989 by John Joseph Crimmins. Reprinted by permission of the author.

David Rollison, from "Outlaw Music," in OUTLAW MUSIC, copyright © 1976 by David Rollison. Reprinted by permission of the author.

Rumi, untitled poem, copyright © 1986 by Threshold Books, RD 3, Box 1350, Putney, Vermont 05346. Reprinted by permission of the author.

John Joseph Crimmins, from "Entering the Unknown," in BLIND CORNERS, copyright © 1989 by John Joseph Crimmins, Paper Boats Press, Los Angeles. Reprinted by permission of the author.

CONTENTS

Wind Horse Woman

The winds
lift us out of remembrance

and into discovery.
The earth begs us

to go outside
like a woman

who has no home
and would ride

some elegiac
dream

into a first heaven
if she could only find

the path.
No one sees the main road any more.

The winds come.
The horse at the edge of the mind

turns to face us
like thunder.

—John Joseph Crimmins

INTRODUCTION

I became an apprentice of Agnes Whistling Elk fifteen years ago. When I was subsequently initiated into the Sisterhood of the Shields, it became clear to me, as the only non-native woman, that I had a special destiny with them. Agnes asked me to write about our life and teaching together. She said that we live in a time of vision, a time when the people of mother earth are eager for a new and more balanced way of life. "First we must heal the body of mother earth with a renewed understanding of feminine consciousness. We must move out into the world to experience what is missing. What is missing is an understanding and incorporation of the primal woman," Agnes said to me with tears in her eyes.

From that day on, I have been working with different members of the Sisterhood on my process of evolvement. I have been sharing my experiences as that process relates to twentieth-century life and survival.

Every fifty years the Sisterhood of the Shields meets in the Valley of Luktang in Tibet. For years I was told of this extraordinary gathering. *Windhorse Woman* is about our journey into Nepal and Tibet.

I have changed the names and places of all those involved. This has been done in all my books to protect their privacy. I am not writing as an anthropologist, but as a woman in search of truth. This book does not illustrate traditional shamanic traditions from Nepal or Tibet. The ceremonies that we perform in all of my books are for a non-native woman and they relate to my specific needs as an apprentice on the path of heart.

The manner and appearance of a prophet,
our secret origins, these are born
of a woman who still lives inside us,
though she's hiding from what we've become.

   —Rumi
      Tr. by John Moyne and Coleman Barks

CHAPTER ONE
SPIRIT WIND

"It has been written in sacred symbols by the Gods, all that will come to pass."

An old Nepalese hill woman with creased mahogany skin and thick gray hair was sitting on her heels in a squatting position. She was stringing large coral beads. She wore a printed red sari and a bright yellow blouse. The woman she was speaking to was not much younger, but seemed to be attending to the older woman's needs, much as an apprentice would do.

"Have some buttered tea, Ani," the younger woman said, placing an earthenware cup on the adobe ledge near her.

Ani was deep in thought, her eyes squinting so that barely a glint of light reflected off her dark eyes. Then taking the cup, Ani looked into it and wrinkled her nose, sniffing the smear of yak butter that was settling on the surface of the tan liquid. Her thoughts had gone beneath the water and tea. All her life, the configuration of simple tea leaves in a cup of tea had stimulated Ani's great gift of prophecy. After a long time she whispered, "Oh, my dear Didi, I have waited all my years for what is soon to come." Ani spoke in Nepalese.

"Ani, what are you speaking of?"

"I have taught you long and well, Didi. Look into the tea water for yourself and you tell me."

Ani, her huge carved silver earrings shining like shields in the sun, handed the tea cup back to Didi. Their brown fingers, hard like weathered goat hide, met for a moment.

Didi looked at Ani with surprise and then slowly lifted the cup with both hands up to gazing level. She took a deep breath, her chest under her heavy bone necklace rising and falling quietly for several moments.

"Oh!" she exclaimed. "As it is written in the caves, what you saw as a young girl in the mountains of Nepal will come to pass!" Now Ani got to her feet, unable to contain her excitement.

"Look Didi, there, that rainbow. It means there is a bridge from one kingdom to another. We have waited lifetimes for the last piece of the mandala to arrive. A young woman will search for us. She will bring us a gift. She does not know the sacred transport of her journey. I must teach her through a long ascent into the mountains of the Chepang."

"You mean she does not know why she is coming to meet with us?"

"No, truth must be passed on through experience. She will bring us a gift that will in some way complete this sacred round. It will be the key to finding the sacred center that has been lost to us for thousands of years. There is a valley high in the Himalayas where the great books are hidden in stone vaults. Many of the teachings have been revealed to us in the sacred hills and in the sky. The ancient ones have showed us many things, but never have they led us to the valley where the lost teachings have been hidden for centuries."

Ani's eyes closed. She was remembering a beautiful vision she had seen as a young girl with her teacher in the mountains. She had run her fingers over the sacred writing on cold cave walls and suddenly a whole world had opened up before her. She had seen a vision of a valley surrounded by high snow-capped mountains, meadows of flowers, and crystal-clear lakes surrounding a beautiful stone monastery with a golden spire. It was a building so beautiful it was unlike any other she had ever seen. For a moment she had a glimpse of a small library within the monastery, and then the vision vanished as quickly as it had appeared.

"Oh, Grandmother, what does it mean?" she had asked her teacher.

"It means that perhaps you will be shown the way to the secret valley. One day it could happen for you, my daughter."

More than ninety years had passed since that day in the caves and yet the memory in Ani's head was as clear as if it had happened the day before. Ani turned and looked at Didi.

"All Asia has spoken of hidden kingdoms like Shambala or Shangri-La. Many have thought her green pastures and citadels of wisdom were desiccated and lost forever. Many see her only as a legend of a possible great city that is now in ruin under the shifting sands of an Asian desert. But they have lost faith. There is a special valley and the sacred knowledge of our ancestors comes from her."

Ani turned away and looked towards the snow-covered Himalayas. The darkness of evening was rising up out of the valley. The purple shadows elongated the deep crevices in the foothills. A hawk circled above, turning gold and then silver as he disappeared into the mist settling over the small stone house. Bells sounded from down the mountain, their tones lasting for many minutes.

"A spirit wind is in the mountains, Didi. The mountains dance for us. They have the spirit we are looking for and they teach us with their circles of stone. Hear them ringing with sound, Didi, like the bells on Vishnu Street or the water spouts at Muktinath."

The two grandmothers smiled at each other with great joy as the mist enshrouded the adobe portal and the entire house was lost in a white cloud.

Dreaming the Roads

Snow leopards
cast about
on their own power
seeking highest air.

It is our right to live
wild as jackrabbits
quick as blue belly lizards
racing near the back porch.

I dream of snowy roads
a great winter coat
obscuring
the road's torso.

And through our shoes,
with eyes found
at bottom of our feet,
we see our way.

—John Joseph Crimmins

CHAPTER TWO
THE WIND
IS LIKE A HORSE

An icy wind blew across the glacier pass. My cheeks were covered with tiny particles of snow that had swirled up from the ice in the blustering wind currents. Dorje Lapka stood golden and austere against the blue purple sky. A sherpa leading a yak, Agnes Whistling Elk, Ruby, Plenty Chiefs, and I trekked around a glacier that had been inching its way ten million years down a slice between sheer gray striated cliffs. Walking over the crest of the path we collectively caught our breath as we looked down into a green valley surrounded by snow-covered Himalayan peaks. Farther down on either side of the trail were tall rhododendron bushes blooming with bursts of garnet red color. The change in vegetation from stark barren windswept glacier country to green flowered meadows and villages was surreal, as if one reality defined the other in a polarity of color and feeling.

We had been walking at a steady pace for over four hours. The trail had been climbing always gently upward. My legs were tired and very sore from the three preceding days. We had been trekking from a small village three days outside of Kathmandu. My head and heart were so full of new smells, sounds, and the magnificent kaleidoscope of mountain and valley grandeur that neither Agnes, Ruby, nor I had been sleeping very well. Every bell sounding or snort from the yak found us wide awake and looking around. Now at the crest of the trail we sat down to rest.

Our sherpa, named Concha, had been very remote and gruff at first, but now was full of smiles. He seemed to have attached himself to Ruby. He was fascinated by her strange blue eyes and the fact that even though blind she could see her way on the mountain paths as well as he. She poked and kidded him and they laughed together like children, his thirty-year-old face as dark as hers, but with many fewer wrinkles. Concha seemed a little in awe of these two old Indian women who looked so oddly young and yet ancient. I would catch him staring at them and then at me as if he were waiting for me to turn into an old crone before his very eyes. Many times I muttered to him that it might not be long, so he should keep on looking, as I struggled up a particularly steep part on the trail with shale shifting under my boots, sending me skidding down on my side for ten or fifteen yards.

I took a sip of water from my canteen and curled up in a sheepskin that Concha offered to me. My thought was just to close my eyes and rest for a few minutes. I still had not totally adjusted to the altitude. Due to my physical exhaustion and the thinner air, I was in a deep sleep in moments, as I felt the wind come up from the valley and fill me with the scent of flowers and newly cut grasses. As I slept, I dreamed of northern Canada and the cabin where I had first met Agnes. I had gone to visit her there a few months ago and our journey to Nepal had been revealed to us at that time in a crystal ceremony. My dreaming on this mountain pass was so vivid it was as if I were physically going back in time. I had sat down with Agnes in her cabin when I first arrived. I remembered I had looked into her face, tears of joy stinging my eyes. She looked so old that the skin on her cheeks had sunk even farther under her rounded cheekbones. She reminded me of a beautiful oak leaf turned brown and fragile with age. I felt that if I touched her at that moment she might crumble and turn to dust.

"Agnes, I have missed you so much," I said. I was sniveling into my Kleenex.

"Have you got allergies, my daughter?"

"No, well, maybe—I just am so glad to see you."

Agnes stoked the fire in the potbelly stove and sat down with a blue and red trade blanket over her legs. She wore her customary Pendelton shirt and a denim skirt. A red and white beaded shield hung from around her neck. She watched me with some amusement. The wind whistled around the corner of the cabin, the logs in the walls creaking. Outside it was twilight, the time when the world changes. There was a stillness about Agnes that was contagious. Soon I stopped fidgeting and put my Kleenex away. I sat down across from this Indian woman who had been my teacher for so many years. It could have been yesterday that I had sat here inquiring about the sacred marriage basket. That was so long ago.

"We have not been together in this cabin for many seasons, my daughter. You have much to tell me," Agnes said. Her eyes were catching the rays of sunset light that filtered through the window across from us. Her eyes began to shine like dusty mirrors, and a faint smile tugged at the corners of her mouth.

"Agnes, why are you smiling at me like that?" She was making me fidget again with her intense gaze. A row of white teeth appeared as Agnes slapped her knee and laughed out loud.

"All these years and an old, broken-down Indian woman still makes you nervous." Her shoulders bounced up and down as she giggled. Then her mood shifted instantly, as I had witnessed so often before.

When a thought crossed Agnes' mind like a cloud traveling over the face of the moon, the light emanating from her eyes would darken and her expression would become serious. When this happened, all I could do was wait respectfully and listen. I never disturbed her thoughts. Now she sat quietly, closing her eyes as if listening to her heart. I closed my eyes too, but my lids wanted to snap open. I wanted to watch the face of my teacher from whom I had been separated for so many months. I loved her and I needed to see her.

"Close your eyes," Agnes said in a soft voice.

I shut my eyes, wondering how she knew they were open. I tried to sit quietly. My nose itched and I scratched my arm that had begun to tingle. I wiggled in my chair and it squeaked and scraped on the board floor of the cabin. Then, try as I might to hold it back, I sneezed. I looked at Agnes and she was glaring at me. I felt like a mouse being watched by a cat.

"Sorry," I said.

Agnes closed her eyes again and I did the same. This time I took a deep breath and began to relax. I listened to the wind moaning outside, and the sound of the high blowing in the fir trees settled me into myself. Finally my excitement at seeing Agnes again calmed into a warm glow of quiet enthusiasm. After several minutes, Agnes spoke.

"It has always been the wind for you."

"What do you mean?"

"The wind is like a horse for you. You ride her into other worlds," Agnes said, looking at me.

"I guess you're right. I hadn't thought of it that way."

"The wind is a relative of yours and an important ally. Let's find out what this ancestor wind has to tell you."

"What do you want me to do?"

"I want you to look into my eyes and think of an old grandmother, a grandmother as old as the North Wind. She is the wind. She is ancient, but she is buoyant and joyous and she plays with the loose fragments of your mind, the ones that have not yet fit into the great puzzle. Let her blow those pieces of thought into a giant whirlwind. Look into my eyes, my daughter, and listen to the wind. She has something to say."

As I looked into Agnes' eyes it grew darker outside. The fire crackled in the stove and the gas lamp flickered and dimmed. Agnes' face became more radiant, and her eyes appeared to glow with an immense energy that seemed somehow separate from her. It was as if another energy form had come to join with hers. A life force was projecting through her eyes that was unfamiliar to me. I was fascinated watching the subtle changes in light around the iris of her eyes. I gazed at her unblinking for a long time. Just as a wave of powerful energy began to move inside of me, Agnes closed her eyes and shifted in her chair.

"That's enough for now, Little Wolf," she said, rubbing her hands together. "Make us some tea and we'll sleep. It is late."

"Agnes, what was that all about? You looked so strange. Your eyes completely changed. I've never seen you do that before." I was rubbing my numbed arms and trying to get my senses back. I got up and made us a cup of tea. I joined Agnes again in front of the wood stove.

"Did you hear the wind talking?" Agnes asked.

"Just now?"

"No, you silly pup, when you were looking into my eyes."

"I guess not really. I was so fascinated by your eyes."

"Next time pay attention to grandmother wind. She has much to tell you about a land far away."

"What land far away?"

"Never mind. I am sleepy. We will talk tomorrow."

Agnes set her cup of tea down on the table. She quickly skimmed off her clothes and slid into bed without another word. I turned down the gas lamp, stoked the fire, and unrolled my old sleeping bag. I was soon lying on my back staring at the quaking shadows on the wood ceiling. I wondered what was in store for me. I felt a mystery lurking very near. Something from Agnes' eyes had pulled me. Was it a message, perhaps, or a person far away trying to communicate with us? I couldn't seem to decipher the meaning of the energy that I had seen there. The next thing I knew it was a sunny, beautiful morning and Agnes was preparing some biscuits for breakfast.

"Hmmm, those smell good," I said, getting up and putting away my bedroll.

As Agnes and I sat at the wooden table having breakfast, we were both unusually silent. Finally Agnes looked at me and stopped eating.

"What did you dream about last night?" she asked.

"I dreamt of high mountains. Now that you ask, it was a strange night. I felt pulled in some inexplicable way. It was almost as if a lover were looking for me in my dreams, but we never found each other. I felt compelled by something, but I don't know what it was."

"Hmmm," Agnes said.

She had picked up one of her small medicine bundles. I watched her brown finger lift a double-terminated crystal out from the red material and hold it up to the morning light. Rainbow colors flashed around the room. Beacons of light picked up the wood smoke hanging in the air, transforming it into plumes of crimson and blue.

"I felt the pull too, my daughter, and I feel it now." Her face had become serious as she peered into the crystal. As often happened with Agnes, she had seen something special in the crystal and would immediately honor it with a ceremony.

"Quickly, my daughter, bring my pouches of cornmeal and tobacco and those crystal pouches over there."

I fetched the pouches and then lit an abalone shell full of silver sage leaves. In moments the air was pungent and heavy with gray swirling sage smoke. I lit several candles and began singing softly with Agnes as we called to the Spirits of the Crystal Dreamtime and announced our sudden ceremony. I don't know how much time passed, but it was a long while before we could focus all of our thoughts so that the spirits of the crystal configurations would enter.

At last Agnes and I were settled into our respective places of power within ourselves. The rainbow light that was emanating from the large crystal that was now enthroned on a mound of cornmeal began to flicker and Agnes took over the ceremony. She peered into the crystalline light as did I. I could see nothing but intense white light. My eyes remained open even though they hurt. Inside my head I heard something like the wind blowing around the corners of the cabin. Then I heard a strange language, one I had never heard before—something between Chinese and East Indian. An old woman's voice was speaking in beautiful low tones. The structure of her intonations and phrasing mesmerized me and calmed me deeply. Before I knew it, I was understanding her words, but I didn't think she was speaking English. I just kind of tuned into the meaning. It was as if she were giving a speech and we came in after she had begun.

She said, "Truth is the only purity. The energy that you have been feeling is a kind of truth; in actuality it is a force. Most people on earth think that the physical world and the spirit world are combined, that they are one and the same. They also think that force or energy is part of the material world and is usually produced by it. Look at your crystal, it is a perfect example. It represents a crystallized form of spirit, because it is of the material realm. Force, on the other hand, is spirit that has not yet been crystallized into a physical form. The rainbows emanating from the crystal are the color of force that is more dense than spirit and not yet a form. The music of the earth mother sings to us through color. When you see form, you see color. And when you see color, you see music and tones in their solid form. The force that has been felt in your dreams is a pervading energy that people the world over are feeling and do not understand. They experience this energy as a quick-ening. Their lives are moving faster and they can barely keep up with their shifts in consciousness and the needs of everyday life. They don't understand that spirit is increasing their needs so that new mirrors can be formed. These mirrors are teachers if only the people will have the courage to look into them and learn. This is a time of great planetary change. Many of the great time calendars are ending now because we are entering a new age of wisdom. We have the possibility of creating a new world of heightened understanding. Many ancient truths will be revealed to you in the coming months. We live in a time of vision. The great libraries of knowledge will be opened to many from different paths and religions. There is much for you to learn, but truth is never reached without struggle on the human path."

The voice faded and a vision replaced the sound of the old woman's voice. The vision was not outside me, but was within my head. I was standing with Agnes at the edge of a lake high in the mountains. There was a raftlike boat tied nearby. It was afternoon and a cool wind was blowing ripples on the blue-green surface of the water. I got into the boat alone and paddled my way across the pond and through the crystal-clear reflection of the craggy snow-covered peaks surrounding me. At the other side, I left the boat. I walked up a path and then up old wooden steps that led to an adobe and stone house sitting in a grove of rhododendron bushes flowering crimson and white. I knocked on the door and waited. I heard bells ringing from across the lake and wondered where this beautiful land existed. I had forgotten the crystal ceremony and Agnes' cabin.

Then slowly the door was opened by an elderly native woman in a red sari skirt and blouse. She asked me to enter. I looked across the room and sitting at a table wearing large silver earrings and a coral necklace was a very old Indian look-ing woman with long gray hair braided back and down behind her shoulders. She wore bright yellow colors and a welcoming smile. I was carrying a small package or bundle wrapped in red material and I placed it as an offering on her table. I was startled because her voice was familiar. It was the same voice from the crystal.

"It is time, my daughter. You have at last arrived in the Kingdom of Nepal. My name is Ani." She spoke carefully now in broken English, with a Nepalese accent. She was familiar to me, but before my eyes could adjust to the dimness in the house the vision was gone and I was back in Agnes' cabin in Manitoba, Canada.

After several minutes I looked across at Agnes, who sat expectantly waiting.

"Well?" She asked as if I had just come home from the store.

"Did you see her, too?" I asked, shaking my head and wiping tears from my eyes as I tried frantically to adjust to present reality.

"Yes, my daughter. And did you not recognize her?" Agnes asked, ignoring my struggle.

"Yes, I thought I knew the woman, but I couldn't really say from where. The inside of her hut was so dark. It all happened so fast."

Agnes smudged her crystal with smoke from a smoldering braid of sweetgrass. With great care and reverence she cleaned the crystals with her hair and mine, and then wrapped them in red felt and placed them back in her medicine bundles. The morning light reflected off the red and blue trade beads sewn in a morning-glory design on the front of the deerskin pouches.

"I know I've seen her before, but how could I—I've never been to Nepal."

"Maybe she visited you someplace else," Agnes said.

"I know you know who she is, Agnes. Why don't you just tell me?"

"Because this is too much fun."

"Agnes, tell me, please."

"I'm going for a walk. In fact I'm going to get some soapstone down at Dead Man's Creek just for you."

"Why just for me? I don't need any soapstone."

"Yes, you do. It's time you learned how to carve."

With that, Agnes grabbed a sweater and left the cabin heading for the "crick" at a fast pace. I followed her onto the porch and then, changing my mind about staying, I ran after her.

"Carve? I don't want to carve. I want to talk about all those things Ani told us. I want to go to Nepal and see her," I said, pulling on Agnes' sleeve and tripping over some poplar branches laying on the path.

"You can't go running halfway around the world to visit someone you don't even know." Agnes laughed at the look of dismay on my face. "Well, you did say you don't remember her, didn't you?" Agnes asked.

"Yes. But I will remember her."

"For now, you're going to learn to carve."

Agnes was already squatting down by the stream, its cold water rushing over her hands and turning them into shimmering, distorted reflections of themselves.

"Agnes, I don't understand why you're being so difficult."

"You will," she said, handing me six or seven flat round stones from the river bottom. I laid them dripping onto the moss that we were now sitting on.

"Close your eyes," Agnes commanded. When she uses that tone of voice I do as she says.

"Place your hands on this tribe of stones and tell me which ones are male or female, and, most important, tell me which one is the matriarch, the old, wise medicine woman."

I had to take several deep breaths from my belly to clear my clamoring thoughts. It took several minutes, but finally I placed my fingers on each of the cool, wet stones.

"This one is male, so is this one. This one is a female."

As I rubbed my fingers over them, their brown surfaces felt a little slimy or soapy. At last a flat stone about six or seven inches square began to speak to me in silence. She was very old. I could sense her age and her wisdom. There was a definite communication between us, but there is no language to explain the depth of well-being that she communicated to me. Finally I opened my eyes. Agnes was still sitting in a deep, quiet state with her eyes closed.

As she opened her eyes Agnes said, "She is a wise grandmother. She gave you a message about silence, my daughter. Did you understand?"

"Only that I felt a depth of spirit."

"Silence is where the Great Spirit lives. He does not live in language. That's why you love animals, nature, and horses so much; because there are no words between you, only silence. You transmit your love for them from the heart and not from your mind in words. In silence there is divinity.

"This grandmother stone is perfect for your sculpting, my daughter. But first you must ask her what form she would enjoy. Like the Great Spirit, you must see the unborn form lying within the stone. You will help it to be brought into this world, by cutting the cocoon of rock that is hiding it. It has wanted to be born for centuries and now she has presented herself to you."

For minutes I stared at Agnes and then at the brownish stone laying in my hands. I had never thought of an unborn form within a stone, but I remembered conversations with sculptors where they had spoken of something like that. But this was different. Through the weight of the stone I began to feel something softer and deeply vibrant. I looked into the stone in a way that made me look more deeply within myself at the same time. A feeling of buoyancy and joy swept over me. For a moment tears came to my eyes, tears of happiness and freedom. A freedom that only the wind or a wild horse knows.

"That's it!" I said. I handed Agnes the stone and jumped up dancing around with excitement. "It's a horse. A beautiful, free, wild horse."

Now it was Agnes' turn to stare. She looked down at the flat, squarish stone and then up at me.

"A wild horse?" she asked, turning the stone in the light.

"Yes, I am sure."

"Okay, if you say so. Personally, it looks like a mugwump to me."

"What's a mugwump?"

"That's a bird sitting on the fence with her mug on one side and her wump on the other." Agnes laughed and poked my ribs.

"Agnes, for heaven's sake," I said, as I giggled and helped her put the other stones back in the water where they had been.

Leaving

If nothing goes on but living
then there is no savageness of day.

Arrived at the hill above the river
across from Pashupatinath temple

as the last smoke was rising
from one cremated body.

At another place on the Bagmati River
a body is wrapped first in red, then

soft yellow, then bright
sun yellow.

The husband and two sons
of a dead woman

have their heads shaved
to signify mourning.

Watching the wood pyre built
yards away from the body at riverbank.

And leaving the hot sun
before the new burning begins.

—John Joseph Crimmins

CHAPTER THREE

A PROCESS OF ALCHEMY

I awoke from my dreaming, startled for a moment, as I realized that I was on a mountain trail in Nepal, and had a sip of tea and a piece of tsampa, a barley breadcake that Concha had prepared. It was not long before we were back on the winding path.

As we carefully chose the placement of each footstep on the ancient slippery slabs of stone set into the steep trail descending from Chorapani Pass, I paused a moment and felt in my backpack for the tiny figure of the wild horse that I had carved. I remembered how the soapstone had almost fallen away under my tools to give birth to a galloping horse. Once carved, I had polished my creation, and Agnes and I had empowered it with many ceremonies and given it tiny crystal eyes chipped carefully from the Mother Crystal so special to the Sisterhood of the Shields. I felt the red silk painted deer hide of the bundle tied with horsehair, knowing it was safe. We continued down the trail.

Annapurna South and Machapuchare, the west Himalayan mountain ranges, and the jutting peak of Dorje Lapka crowned the horizon line above the green valley of Luktang like a shimmering diamond tiara. Dorje Lapka glowed as if the brilliant sun were shining from within her and she herself were the source. Crystalline light penetrated every delicate leaf and flower in the fields ahead of us. The view was so awe-inspiring that we would forget our struggle with the altitude and with our bodies that were aching and so tired. There were several lookout points along the way, and finally we stopped at one. We were so happy for a chance to rest that we gratefully ate the rice and tea that Concha prepared. We sat in silence. Ruby rested against a round stone and was instantly asleep.

Hearing laughter, Agnes and I looked back up the trail to see two young Europeans, young lovers, trekking towards us. For a moment their lips met in a quick kiss; then they saw us. Blushing with embarrassment, they ran by us, holding hands and waving. They spoke German hellos to us then disappeared around a turn in the path. I was aware that Agnes was looking at me with a quizzical expression.

"What?" I asked.

"You were thinking something when you saw those young lovers," she said.

"I guess I was."

"Well?"

"I was thinking about energy."

"What kind of energy?" Agnes asked through a big smile.

"Sexual energy, I guess, like those kids had. I have always had a lot of sexual energy, but it changed somehow awhile ago."

"How do you mean—changed?"

"Well, it feels different." I thought for a while as I sipped tea and looked out across the valley at Annapurna Himal. "It's much quieter and less agitated."

Agnes picked up two stones and felt them with her fingers, rolling them over and over. "What happened is that you use your sexual energy differently than you used to, my daughter. When you first became my apprentice you had hot pants for everything—knowledge, sex, you name it."

"Agnes!" I exclaimed at her comment.

"Hey, for once you're talking about something interesting," Ruby said, opening an eye and scratching her nose.

Agnes ignored Ruby and went on. "Understand me, Lynn, all young people have hot pants. They don't know how to channel and use that energy effectively. Our early training for a woman of power is to train her to focus all of her energy and to help her understand that its source is sexual. When you regained the marriage basket, do you remember what I told you?"

"You told me many things."

"I told you that the marriage basket was woven from the dreams of all women. I told you that the basket belonged to a medicine society of women called the Dreamers, or the Sisterhood of the Shields. Part of your initiation into our Dreaming Society was learning how to Dream well enough to take the basket away from the sorcerer who had stolen it. Do you remember?" Agnes was chewing on a blade of grass. Ruby was asleep again.

"How could I forget?" Flashes of a bearded sorcerer and the basket encircled by luminous fibers danced through my mind.

"When you focus your energy in such ways you enlist the power and knowledge of your body mind. It is located, as you know, around your navel. In the world of shamanism we call this your intent, or your ability to transform your energy into other forms such as Dreaming. You have always been acclimated to Dreaming because of your powerful sexual drive. When you first held the marriage basket and its spiritual essence became part of your own belly, you were changed forever. Your destiny became entwined with the dreams of all women. Just like the fibers of the basket were woven into a subtly beautiful pattern, so were the designs of your soul blended with the patterns of the lives of all women. In a sense you became one with them. You also became a Dreamer capable of traversing many dimensions, shaman dimensions of healing and light. You need energy for that. That energy begins with sexual energy. That is why you now have a different sense of your own sexual drive. It is still there, but it is used in many different ways now, so it feels different, very different."

Sometimes there was a little-girl part of me that wanted to scream out at Agnes as if I had been victimized in some way, but another inner voice knew better. The voice of the new woman I have become knows that I had made a bid for knowledge long ago, and that if my body and spirit were alchemized, as surely they must be in this process of transformation, then so be it.

The Young Rider

Not waiting for any command
nor permission, she rides, hair flying,
wind acknowledging, yes.

I have come to teach you the basics
she said to me, holding her hand over mine,
gently placing my fearfulness, replacing

my fear, in long deep smooth handstrokes
on the gray horse's mane. The horse stretches with joy
unable to scratch here himself.

In my mind this young one is always riding.
She carries some abandoned spirit,
purposeful in her determination,

a longing, the will
to ride free, curling into, leaning into
the turn

where the horse glimpses
a memory
of his ancestor's desert

and the young one
senses the world
where together they are leaping.

I, we, who watch,
perceive
and almost go along.

—John Joseph Crimmins

CHAPTER FOUR

THE SEED OF LIFE

Fifteen minutes later we were back on the trail. We all felt refreshed and set off at a good pace. But as we rounded a jagged corner of the mountain a blast of cold air welcomed us with a dense white cloud of fog. We could not see twenty feet in front of us. The valley below was completely obscured from view. Concha asked us if we wanted to stop and wait out the fog. We decided we wanted to be into the valley by dark, so we walked close together, inching our way like a caterpillar, down through the cotton-candy–looking clouds.

By the end of two hours a stiff wind had blown most of the fog into a canyon to the south. We found ourselves on a low ridge above the end of a long valley with the Langtang Khola River shimmering like a satin ribbon in the distance.

"There." Agnes pointed to a small lake surrounded by wheatfields with a small adobe and rock house at its edge. That's where we're going." Agnes started off down the trail.

I had been leading the yak, who had not been happy with the fog. I gave her lead to Concha and caught up with Agnes. Concha and Ruby followed behind.

"Those lakes in the distance," Agnes pointed out, "were

25

created by Shiva—it is told in legend—thrusting his trident into the mountain and producing three springs. Those springs feed the lakes. This is a very holy valley."

"Agnes, I've been here before," I said. I grabbed her arm and made her slow down.

"Does that really surprise you?" she asked, still walking.

"Yes, well, not exactly. It scares me. You knew that was the house I saw through the crystal ceremony in your cabin. Is Ani going to be there also?"

"Yes. This is an important day. At the fork up ahead we'll say goodbye to Concha and then I will show you what to do," Agnes said.

When we reached the fork in the trail, we all gathered and had tea together. We fed the yak, whom I loved, green grass that we gathered. Concha called her Bengal Bay and we patted and kissed her goodbye. We were in tears when we said good-bye to Concha. He and Ruby said they hoped to meet again later. In a short time, Concha had begun to feel like family. We waved farewell as he headed up another trail leading to a base camp at the foot of Dorje Lapka. We watched them disappear around the end of the ridge. I looked back at the lake and house only an acre away. The wheatfields, terraced and serene, lay under a subtle golden mist. The sense of light and the warm temperature was like my vision. I felt very strange, as if my understanding of reality was being challenged by some unseen dimension. I pinched myself to make sure I wasn't still dreaming.

"No need to mutilate yourself," Ruby said. "You're not dreaming." She sat down at the edge of the clear lake as soon as we reached it. Taking off her shoes, she placed her feet in the shallow margin of water. She straightened her legs and splashed her feet like a little girl. Next to her was a small raftlike boat. I sat down next to Agnes and stared at her.

"I've always told you that what you imagine is real," Agnes said, holding up a small quail's egg that she had found in the grass. "The yolk of this egg is like your vision of Ani. Your vision held the seed of the promise of life. For this life to actually manifest it must have nourishment. It needs to be fed to exist. Your coming here now is like the white of this egg. Through your effort and trust and energy, magic is about to be created.

For the seed of life, the yolk to be born, it must have you. Take out your horse carving."

I did as Agnes instructed. Before I knew it, I was alone in the boat and paddling my way towards the house. It was exactly the same time of day as before and a new cool wind was blowing ripples on the blue-green surface of the water. I could see Dorje Lapka and the snowy Himalayas reflected all around me. As I walked up the old wooden steps, I noticed that the crimson and white rhododendrons were bursting with flowers. I knocked on the blue-painted door as I heard bells ringing across the valley. A cold fear that had been crawling up my spine dissipated as the door was opened by an elderly Nepali woman wearing a red sari skirt and shirt.

"Namaste," she said, welcoming me in. I thought I saw tears in her eyes as she turned away and led me across the room. At a table, looking at me, was Ani. She had long gray hair braided back and down behind her shoulders. Her large silver earrings caught the afternoon sun. She wore a bright yellow sari. I placed my offering on the table and sat in the chair that she indicated by a nod. My offering was wrapped in red silk.

"It is time, my daughter. You have at last arrived in the Kingdom of Nepal. Namaste. My name is Ani."

"Namaste," I managed to whisper as the other woman served us tea and said, "Namaste, I am Didi."

"Thank you, Didi. I am Lynn."

Ani picked up the small offering with tenderness. She held it to her heart before opening it. Her face was mahogany-brown and terraced with wrinkles like her wheatfields. Her eyes sparkled with anticipation as she let the red silk fall away. Her eyes widened and her mouth dropped open as she held the carving up to the light.

"A wild horse, fast as the wind," she said.

"It's one of my first carvings. I wish it were more perfect."

"Yes, yes, you have a word for wild horses. You call them . . . ?" She struggled to find the word.

"Mustang," I said.

"Of course, Mustang! In the district of Mustang! Then it must be Windhorse," she muttered to herself.

"Excuse me?" I asked, not hearing her.

"Oh nothing, you have brought me a beautiful Mustang. I am so grateful."

She looked at me. Tears filled her eyes. I didn't understand why she was so excited about my carving. Ani must have read my expression.

"Forgive me, my daughter. Your transport of this carving has been a sacred journey. You have successfully followed your vision and delivered to me the awaited key. I have been waiting for you all my life."

"But it's just a carving of a wild horse. Are you sure . . . ?" I stopped speaking.

Ani's eyes were scanning me with such intensity that I was speechless. I remembered the vision, and I realized that Ani was part of the Sisterhood of the Shields. I realized that what she was telling me was true. Ani and Didi got up and gave me tearful hugs. I was filled with happiness and was completely confused. There was a knock on the door. Didi hurried to open it. Agnes and Ruby entered carrying a bundle of white flowers. The women hugged and kissed and patted each other late into the night as we ate and laughed together. None of us could hold back the tears of joy at being reunited. Ani placed my proud little carving on her house altar in the corner of the room and lit a mustard-oil lamp beside it so we could see it. Didi put several blossoms at the horse's feet. Later in the evening as we prepared for sleep, Ruby came around the table to sit next to me on a bench.

"Do you still think you are dreaming, little wolf?" Ruby said, her face in profile to me, her eyes reflecting a cloudy blue.

"No," I said, feeling instantly nervous as I always did when Ruby approached me in this way.

"You carved a pretty good horse there, Lynn."

"Thank you, Ruby."

"Do you know what it means to have Horse Magic?"

"No, not exactly."

"It means that you learn to merge with the soul of a horse so you can share his abilities and share his exalted being. A horse has a swiftness of spirit."

"Oh. That's wonderful," I said, not knowing what else to say.

Ruby giggled to herself and patted me on the head as she got up and unrolled her cotton mat to prepare for sleep.

"That swiftness may be important to you one day. You may need it to survive. Perhaps you should learn more about it," Ruby said as she rolled over on her side.

"What do you mean, I might need it to survive?" I hated the way Ruby always scared me. Now how could I sleep? I could hear Ruby's even breathing, which meant she was already asleep. Agnes and Ani winked at me as they chuckled to themselves.

I want there to be no trace.
What remains

should be only substance,
the hard stone,

with complete rivers washed
over its body like a shattered

puzzle. What is left behind
is no longer stone, is no longer

substance, is fine dust
that has settled elsewhere

and is gone. Let the remaining hours
tighten the weave in me.

—John Joseph Crimmins

CHAPTER FIVE

THE WAY OF
THE POWER
HOLDERS

$\mathbf{A}$ni got me up at daybreak to go for a walk. The morning mist covered the ground in wispy cotton white patches. Ani and I walked through one island of cloud to another as if we were sleepwalking in a dream. Ani wore large silver earrings that tinkled subtly as she moved. At one point Ani reached for my hand and turned me to face her. The bottom half of our bodies had disappeared in the mist. We giggled and touched the cloud with our open palms as if it were the head of a favorite dog.

"You should know something about the way of the 'power holders,' my daughter. Before I show you around, I want you to know where my spirit lives."

"When you say the 'power holders,' do you mean a political group?" I asked.

Ani's expression was one of deep thought as her eyes stared off down the mountain through a clearing in the fog.

"In India, Nepal, and Bhotia or Tibet, whenever a religion comes into power, those people band together in a common thought form and create a political force. These forces are often at odds with others, and many innocent people suffer in the name of one god or another. It is like a snow leopard who wakens from a long winter sleep and finds one of her paws in a trap."

"How is that, Ani?"

"If you imagine that our sacred body, our spirit, that has always been free and able to experience its source through its own innate goodness suddenly is trapped in a vise, what do you think happens?"

"You would, or your spirit would, become violent and would want to get away," I said.

"Yes, the thought form—this new idea, shall we say—this religion creeps up while you are sleeping and imprisons you so that you cannot escape. You are caught like a snow leopard in a trap. You are caught by family, by society, by the beliefs of a village that you may live in. Perhaps you take the easy path and cut off your leg and live the rest of your days as a cripple. Or perhaps you fight for freedom, as I have done. I learned how to dismantle the trap and live in freedom. But like the snow leopard, I have had to hide and disguise myself to escape extinction as a species. Like the snow leopard, I can no longer roam freely through my territory. I endured great pain until I learned the workings of the trap, and now no one must ever know that I've escaped."

"But can't they see that you have gone?" I asked, watching Ani's face as her eyes narrowed to slits of yellow light not unlike the leopard she spoke of.

"You, my daughter, will see me as few ever have. I am a jhagrini woman from the Manang District and the land of the blue sheep. My family followed the salt-trade routes of the mountains and into the lowland valleys of Nepal for trade in the colder months. On one of these journeys, when I was very young, I became ill with a disease that would have left me dead or deformed. My father put me with another family to die or to be healed by a grandmother who lived there. We were very poor and my own family had to return to their home, but I was much too sick to make the journey. The grandmother who healed me was a jhagrini woman and a 'power holder.' It took her two years to heal me completely. As I lay in a coma, she worked her miracles of curing. She took me to the land of the dead and returned with me. She illuminated my being and restored the health and freedom of my spirit. She became my teacher and taught me the workings of the trap. She taught me to be invisible in everyday life. If you ask the people of the village who I am, they will say, 'Ani, a good woman who minds her sheep.' "

Ani looked at my concerned expression and patted my hand. Her fingers felt hard and rough like the bark on a tree. She chuckled under her breath, making her shoulders jiggle up and down.

"Come sit on this stone with me and I will explain a little about the power holders."

We had climbed to the top of a grassy hill covered with yellow flowers. The fog had dissipated slightly, revealing the glistening crest of Dorje Lapka in the distance. A cool breeze was coming from the north carrying the scent of pine. I lifted my pashmina shawl up under my chin and snuggled into its warmth.

"Many long time ago, maybe even forty thousand years ago, the people of the lands of Asia were followers of the woman's line. We lived in a matriarchy and the original practitioners of what is now called tantra were women. They were Tantrika women and they were called Vratyas, or 'the holders of power.' These women passed down their knowledge from one generation to another of apprentices and daughters. [Tantrika is like all things that speak about being or living within the true self. A true experience of being comes from the sacred center within your circle and all points on that circle are equidistant from the center.] That is why when the 'people of the sky' from the north lands invaded the south that Tantrika was taken over by the patriarchal system."

"But why, Grandmother?"

"Because with the Vratyas there was no hierarchy. They were the peaceful ones of the earth. The people of the sky stole the female wisdom, distorted it, snuck up on the sleeping snow leopard and imprisoned her paw in a trap. The entire face of Tantra was changed to fit a new thought form called the religions of the patriarch. There are many women today, I have heard, who do not like the idea of a woman having extraordinary powers. Many women themselves want to ignore their special powers, or Shakti energy, and many women allow their Shakti to be rerouted by the male systems that surround them."

Ani spoke with such gentleness in her tone. Seldom did the spark of humor leave the corners of her mouth or the softness of her eyes. Her words were precisely formed, almost as a child would speak. Most of the "r's" were missing from her words.

"How do you mean that male systems reroute Shakti energy?"

"Your societies move Shakti into a great commercialism around physical beauty and glamour, as you say it. In the East there are harem cultures, and everywhere there is prostitution, both mental and physical, of the power of woman. In all of this, sacredness and the female rites of passage have long been forgotten by most. You have been blessed, my daughter, and you have worked hard. You are learning about the ancient systems of initiation for the Great Mother. Without these systems of female knowledge our dear mother earth would no longer live, hmmm?"

"Yes, Ani."

"So back to the invasion by the people of the sky, who came warring to the south. They were Indo-Europeans who invaded India around five thousand years ago. They conquered the Goddess-oriented societies and destroyed the culture of the Dravidians, or the 'people of the earth and of the serpent,' who were considered dark, evil, and inferior on every level. The Dravids had dark skins and worshipped the Cow Goddess of India, or Danu. The people of the sky, or the lighter-skinned Aryans, worshipped the god Indra. In the mythology of India, Indra murdered Danu and her son Urta, who are often described as serpent-demons and then later as the dead cow and calf. Then it is said that the cosmic waters flowed and were pregnant."

Ani chewed on a piece of grass and looked out over the now sunlit valley. Every leaf and stone reflected silvery glints of intense light.

"What do you mean the cosmic waters were pregnant?" I asked.

"They said they were pregnant with the blood of Danu and Urta, giving birth to the sun. What that really means is that the patriarchal caste system was born with the lighter Brahmans, of course, at the top."

Ani picked up a stick, placing one end in the ground. She walked her fingers to the top, as if walking up a ladder, and then she let the stick fall.

"So there you have it, that's how the racial purity system

began. Women were placed under vast restriction. The Muslims later introduced 'purdah,' or domestic harems. The Brahmans were always considered pure and the darker ex-followers of Danu were considered the Untouchables. It is the Brahmans who become the priests and who preside over the temples. It is the ancient Dravidians who clean the toilets. And it came to pass that the Brahmans thought themselves even twice-born. They are also born from the father. You see then the source of 'suttee,' as they call it in India, or the ritual burning of widows and child marriages. The dowries always reverted to the priesthood. That is the result of woman being treated as property."

"Forgive my ignorance, Grandmother, but how is it that everywhere I travel around this great mama"—I placed my fingers on the earth—"I find legends of the Matriarch giving over or being conquered by the Patriarch around the same time in history about three thousand years ago."

Ani now took the stick she had been fiddling with and broke it over her knee. A resounding crack filled the silence of the valley.

"Remember that, whether you believe me or not, remember we choose to come onto this earth to become enlightened. This physical body provides a great opportunity. When we are in the dimension of Spirit it is obvious that the physical dimension can give us a chance to erect and choose mirrors through family work and life situations. It is with these mirrors that enlightenment becomes possible. The power holders know this. You and I will journey together for a while. As it has been for centuries, we have memorized the ancient wisdom of the Vratyas. I will teach you, my daughter, as you will teach me, one mirror reflecting the other." Ani paused for a moment, tilted her head to one side and made a quiet purring sound. "Do you understand better where I come from?"

"I think so." I started to ask her one of many questions that clamored for expression, but Ani had risen and was already several strides down the path toward the stone hut.

"It is good," she called back as I struggled to unkink my ankles and catch up with her.

Later that evening I sat down with Agnes at the wooden table where we often ate together. I was nearing my moon and I was filled with misgivings. Agnes reached across the table and placed her hand over mine. We were in Nepal, but we could have been in her cabin in Manitoba. An oil lamp burned low on the table, casting giant shadows on the close walls, turning the small room into a cache of legendary shapes and figures that silently flickered and swayed from one side to the other.

"This is not an easy path," I said with a great sigh.

"I warned you long ago of the dangers." Agnes' skin had turned a deep mahogany color in the soft light.

"But, in those days, Agnes, there was nothing I couldn't do in the search for knowledge." I stared into the gaslight, close to tears.

"What do you think you can't do?"

From my peripheral vision I could see Agnes' mouth twitch in a slight smile as if she were indulging a small child.

"Right now I feel like I can't do anything."

"You feel overwhelmed with your task?"

"Yes, how did you know?"

Agnes laughed and then she said, "I often feel overwhelmed when I think about what it is taking to bring the earth back into balance. There is so much work to be done. When you sit down to write a book about our experience, I bet dollars to doughnuts you don't think of completing the book in its entirety. Rather, you think of your work a page at a time, and slowly, page by page, the book takes form. Am I right?"

"Yes, Agnes, but how in heaven am I going to write all of what is happening here and make it believable? Nepal is so different from what most people are accustomed to."

"You can only write events as they happen. That is all you have been asked to do. Yes, the events are powerful, fantastic, and other-worldly. But much of what makes up the fabric of truth cannot be touched or proved.

Body Music

And for me
quieter than the religious dawn

holding onto prisms
that divine the source

of knowledge, the world,
the long sleep of dreams,

subtle wordings that reflect our time
like a belly of noise.

—John Joseph Crimmins

CHAPTER SIX

SACRED
SPECTATOR

We followed a young boy herding two sheep down the path. In the distance the Machapuchare mountain range appeared dusty-pink and purple beneath a sapphire-blue sky. The peaks of the Himalayas were white-capped, making the brown and lavender hills in the foreground even more stark; each crevice was edged in yellow light. As always, I struggled to keep up with Ani. As we made a swift descent into a lush green valley with a ribbon of turquoise water dividing its pastures, Ani would look behind and laugh at me as I slipped and slid on the soft footing. The boy and his sheep took a right fork in the path and disappeared over a grassy hill. Ani led us straight on down toward the creek.

"Are you tired, my daughter?" Ani asked, slowing her pace as the path leveled.

"Yes, Ani." I smiled at the twinkle in her eyes. The way the sunlight illuminated her face, she looked for a moment like an animated old and gnarled oak tree. The deep brown creases in her face and hands looked like thick bark.

"When you walk, try to stand straighter, Lynn. The mother," Ani pointed to the earth, "pulls you downwards so you won't fly away. It's part of her relationship with you. It's

41

one way that she expresses her love for you. But, as in all love relationships, the gift of love can create a feeling of bondage unless we learn how to give and take within the laws of that relationship. In your agreement with the mother, in this case, you must learn to stop fighting her."

"But, I'm not fighting her."

"Then why are you so tired?"

"Because you're going so fast."

"Really. But I'm not tired." Ani was laughing.

"Well, you're used to the altitude and . . ."

"You are fighting with the pull of the mother, but you're not aware of what's happening. You're in a fight, and the faster you go the more you fight. It's the fight that makes you tired. Be aware of this and don't lean forward or backwards and you'll be happier." Ani reached out and pushed me gently backwards to a more upright position.

"Come join me over here and we'll rest." Ani motioned toward the river bank beneath a leafy tree. We spread a thin red dhaka shawl that she had been carrying. We sat quite comfortably under the low-slung branches. The direct sun had become very warm. Ani sat easily in a lotus position, her fingers touching. I imitated her.

"Have you always sat in this position, Ani?"

"Why do you ask?" Ani was gazing at the creek water rushing by us.

"Agnes has always taught me to sit with my legs to one side." Ani smiled and kept her eyes on the water. "I guess I was wondering about the Buddhist influence," I said. I, too, began to watch the water. Its movement and sound were refreshing.

"We have always sat in this way. We pay respect to the mother by sitting with our bodies in a circle. It is more efficient this way, because it preserves your energy. And more than that, your body becomes a silent prayer. You sit in a continuous round of energy and then slowly you become the center of that circle of energy. Do you see what I mean?"

"Yes, Grandmother, I can feel that the circle is not broken anywhere."

"Good, my daughter, now close your eyes. Breathe in the mountain air. See her entering green like the meadows that surround us and breathe out crystal blue like the waters. In and out, that is good." After a few minutes she asked, "Now tell me, where is your consciousness?"

I reflected for several minutes. "My consciousness is in my middle."

"Good. And now where is your middle?"

After a moment I touched my naval area. "Somewhere here," I said. "But it feels more like a space."

"Yes. Not your mind, not your belly, but the emptiness within your spirit center. It is very simple. It is a prayer. Your current cannot be lost through your toes or your fingers when you are a circle. Everything comes from a circle."

We sat in silence, listening to the sound of running water.

"When I say holding your power, your energy field, it is another way of saying that you are a female warrior. It is part of your learning."

Several minutes passed as we sat quietly breathing and listening to the fecund sounds of nature everywhere around us. A family of birds in the top of the tree were fending off a chattering bandit squirrel.

"Open your eyes, Lynn, and watch the river flow. The shaman path has many turns. Oftentimes you have climbed mountains on this path, only to drop down on the other side. From me you will learn about your receptive powers. We will travel an interior landscape. You will find nothing and you will go nowhere."

"What shall I do, Grandmother?"

"I want you to do nothing. Watch the river flow."

I watched the river for a long time. Branches floated by. Leaves and an occasional piece of driftwood went on their way. I was having a hard time sitting still.

"How do you feel?" Ani asked.

"Honestly?"

"Yes."

"I'm nervous. Sitting still is difficult for me."

"Try something different. Again you are fighting. A warrioress' path is truly right for you. I can tell much about you and your life by the way that you 'watch.'"

"What do you mean?" I was a bit indignant at the way she could look into me.

"You have been trained by your life conditioning to defend

yourself, your spirit. It has been your only way to survive. Now I'm going to teach you a different way to preserve your spirit. It is so simple that it is very hard, my daughter, so breathe deeply and try to relax." Ani poked me in the ribs playfully. "You are not supposed to do anything. I want you to become what we call the 'sacred spectator.' Our word for this is similar to the meaning of 'mountain.' I want you to try again. This time watch the river flow as if you were a mountain. Be serene, at ease, and totally within your power. Like a mountain you are a sacred spectator."

I watched the water change color as it rippled over the yellow and black stones beneath its turbulent surface. Hours passed and the sun moved in the sky creating different hues of gold, pink, and blue in the current. At first I was frantic to move. Then something began to happen. A peace settled within me and I became quiet. For a long time I was conscious of my breathing, and then there was only the river. My body and mind receded. If a thought came up, I let it go like a branch coming into view and passing out of sight on the surface of the water. I watched until Ani broke the silence.

"See, you have nothing to do. The river minds its own business, yes?"

"Yes, Grandmother."

"Can you describe what you're feeling?"

"I feel separate from the river. As if I'm a mountain watching it flow around my feet. I feel like a witness, somewhat removed and simply watching. Everything is going on around me, madly active in a circular fashion and I am at the center, still and unmoving. What is most important is that my body is still and my spirit is also still. An emptiness began to envelope me. A space opens up like a giant cervix and I am pulled into a womblike space. I float for a long time in emptiness. I am not joyous, nor unjoyous, just empty, I guess."

"Yes, yes, my daughter, it is good." Ani's face beamed. "You see, the most important thing, for now, is that the sacred spectator is separate from the crowd, or from the whirlwind of life experience. To become the witness you must give away your mind. It is a shaman art that you will learn soon enough."

I looked up as a giant hawk flew above us. I pulled my coat on as a cold wind circulated down from the hills. The sun was now low on the horizon.

"Come, it will soon be cold. We must go home and meet with the others."

Ani gave me a big squeeze and pinched my cheek as we started up the trail. "Remember that there is only one thing in life that is constant and unchanging."

"What is that, Ani?"

"It is the sacred spectator." Already the ascent up the winding path was proving more arduous than the descent. I was trying not to puff and blow like a tired packhorse.

"But the mind is ever changing. Doesn't witnessing have something to do with the mind?"

"Not any more than this path has to do with this stone." Ani picked up a brown stone and tossed it off into some tiny blue flowers. "The sacred spectator is part of your very nature. Your mind is a tool, but that is quite another matter. Your mind is a storehouse of valuable information, but you don't think with it. You think out here." Ani held her hands a foot away from her head. "To truly witness with the stance of a sacred spectator is to dissolve the sense of mind completely and live totally in your nature."

"Yes, Grandmother."

Even though I was fascinated by the conversation, I wanted to stop talking, so she wouldn't be aware of me fighting my way up the trail. Try as I might I couldn't stand more erect. I felt like I would fall off the mountain.

"Lynn, here, I'll walk behind you in case you fall."

I was surprised as Ani deftly spun around my laboring body and took up the path behind me. She was laughing and prodding me with her walking stick. I could only laugh at how she heard my thoughts and herded my every step.

Reclamation

From the south window you watch
the morning sun soften frost
on a car parked below, the cold
a brightness almost tangible, as you lean
toward the glass thinking of something else
the alchemist's fire
that burns away an old shell of self
so you find your nascent skin tender and raw.
There was no way to know
you would burn so readily, so greedily.
At first it seemed safe

to be set afire. Later the danger
caught your heart like a kite
and flung it far beyond the horizon.
Now there is no way to know
where it will end. Now there is nothing left
but the simple truth of what you are.
You open your hands to the light.
They are almost transparent. Your fingers—
a revelation, luminous and strange
as the pale translucent roots
of the bulbs you planted in pebbles in the glass
vase, tangled, urgent, and driving the green shoots
toward light.

—Elizabeth Herron

CHAPTER SEVEN
SPIRIT LANGUAGE

At Ani's house there was always the sound of Didi, Ani, or one of us doing some domestic activity. We would often awaken to the muffled scraping of Didi plastering by hand the front steps, portal, and interior floors with a mixture of red clay they call moto. One of us was often taking the wooden churn and clomping with the stick through the yak butter and the dark black tea. The tea was the strongest brew I had ever had and if I hadn't been careful it would have kept me up for days. Sweeping was never ending, nor were the sounds of a pan scraping over a fire grate with the preparation of tsampa, or barley cakes. Ani and Didi both made quiet chucking sounds when they found something that needed to be tended to. Between the birds outside, and the bells and the wind, there was a cacophony of nourishing household rhythm.

Ani's house was made of stone and adobe with a thatched roof. A small square skylight between the log rafters admitted a blaze of golden light. The walls and floor were tinged with a soft lavender, the color of afternoon. Oftentimes Didi would unstack multicolored cotton quilts and rugs and overlay them on the floor. Agnes, Ruby, and I sat on rolled-up cotton mats on the floor and propped our backs against a corner wall. A split white curtain was turning powder blue in the waning light and was held open on both sides by a metal spike set into the adobe. The paned wooden windows were painted a pale yellow and were still open to the day. The windows opened a foot above a level mantle where a peacock-blue metal teapot and several tin plates rested holding a folded towel.

I lay down on my unrolled quilted mat. I stared at the ceiling, trying to settle my mind. For several days, I had wanted to go do something, take a walk, go back down to the river, but Ani had made it clear that I was "to stay put," as she said. She meant in the house. Agnes and Ruby had been having a spirited discussion about how the practice of Mahakala' was similar to the shaman traditions that we had learned about in other parts of the world.

"When they put on that red and black hat and merge with Mahakala', the deity itself, it is the same thing as becoming one with our medicine," Agnes said, stamping her foot at Ruby, who was refusing to agree.

"Agnes, my dear, your medicine is hardly like the highest of the high."

They both got up to continue their discussion outside. As they walked through the doorway I heard Agnes retort with a snort and a jerk on her knitted shawl.

"Ruby, by now you should know that you cannot compare one thing to another, especially deities or sacred entities. Mahakala' is considered the highest of the high, not unlike our Great Spirit. What I'm interested in is that they conjure him and he enters their sacred ceremonial circle. This is very familiar work."

I still lay on my back, feeling ready to explode with unexpressed energy.

"How's the little Black Wolf?" Ani asked, sitting down on her heels beside me and offering me some buttered tea. She walked so silently I hadn't heard her approach. I jumped at the sound of her quiet voice.

"I was listening to Agnes and Ruby argue about Mahakala'," I said.

"Ummm." Ani looked at me and sipped her tea.

"Do you really invoke the deities in the Mahakala' ceremonies?"

"That's one way of saying it," she said.

After several minutes of feeling a serene warm breeze blow in through the window, I asked her, "How would you say it?"

"I would say that I am water and the Mahakala' is water and we flow into each other and become one."

The soft wind blew a fringe of gray hair into her eyes. She swept it back with her hand, which was so large and callused it was more like a paw. I had not realized that her hand was almost as large as her whole face. Her bare feet were large and callused also, giving the appearance of a very old and weathered doll. Her sweetness and tranquility filled the room and I began to relax.

"Ani, if I could always live with you I would be forever calm." We laughed as we heard Agnes and Ruby outside still arguing.

"They're both right, you know?"

"How do you mean, Ani?"

"I am always opposed to you."

"You are?" I sat up now.

"If I am in relation to you, then I am meaningful. If I left you, then you would be meaningless or I would be meaningless. My power holder, my teacher, said that nothing exists, that there is no 'I' because 'you' are everything or you, like water flows into water, you dissolve into all existence and become one with 'everything.' "

"I'm not sure I follow you, Grandmother."

"Every statement a person makes is a partial truth, never a total truth. The opposite of that truth is also partially true. No expression is complete."

"But then how can we talk about truth?"

Ani folded a scarf that lay in front of her on a red-flowered quilt. "You can only express truth with your being, not in words. You are truth. But humans love to talk and argue. It is our favorite addiction. Ruby and Agnes may as well be eating chocolate out there under the tree for the good it will do them. The difference between them and most people is that they know it. That's play for them."

"Is there more than one kind of expression?"

"Yes, positive and negative, two sides of the same coin." Ani flipped a silver rupee onto the quilt with her thumb.

"So, both sides complement one another?"

"Yes, one side cannot exist without the other. It has always been that way. So if you are Buddhist and you work towards nirvana, the absolute state of nothingness, or if you are Hindu and you esteem the state of the Brahma, or the all-knowing total, it is all the same. Both describe an experience that is part of the whole. In other words, if you immerse yourself in emptiness, you begin to know emptiness, yes?"

"Yes, I understand."

"Here, take this little stone. Close your eyes and feel it." Ani threw a small gray stone into my hand. I felt its smooth cool surface between my fingers.

"Go into the stone, experience her quiet soul. The stone welcomes your visit." After several minutes she said, "Let the stone move into you. Open yourself. Let her experience the inside of your heart. See how you are a mirror for each other. You are everywhere mirroring everything. The stone absorbs you and you absorb the stone. How can you be alone if you are everything? And yet, because you are everything, you are totally alone. If you are the totality of existence, then how could anything upset you?"

"I guess I understand, but I don't know that yet in my heart."

"Yes. Well put." Ani placed the back of her hand over my heart. "You had a conversation with the stone, a true communion, yes?"

"Yes, I think so."

"The only true communion is without words. Language is a barrier between us, but we need to talk for many reasons, not necessarily to understand much. Silence is the only true source of communication, like you and the stone. You communed with each other from the essence of yourself. Form was the only difference between you, but that is a matter for another day. I know you and Agnes have moved into the mysteries of silence many times. I want you to see the agreements we make, the links in the chain that represent the way we think we give and take knowledge; how we move from one end of that chain to the other. Do you have more knowledge at the end of a lifetime of linking one thought to another, or do you just end up at the end of the chain, like you started?"

Her question did not require an answer, at least not at that moment. She motioned for me to follow her outside. Agnes and Ruby were still going at it. Ani cupped her hands over my ears and whispered. Following her instructions, I sat on a low stool under a flowering rhododendron bush. The sunlight slanting through the crimson blossoms was radiant. I was immersed in a red glow. I closed my eyes and did as I was told. I found my power center within me. It is located around my navel area. Then I thought of the sky, the flowers, the crystals, and the mountains, trying to determine what language they spoke. As I was doing this, Ani asked me to peripherally hear Agnes and Ruby and think about communication.

"Do you know that there are more than four thousand languages on earth?" Ani asked Agnes.

"Well, it's obvious that Ruby doesn't even know one!" Agnes hissed.

"But you're both encased in your own language," Ani said.

"We started out speaking English and ended up in pig-Latin!" Ruby snorted.

"Ruby, do you want something to drink?" Agnes asked.

"Not from you!"

Agnes stormed into the house. She returned with a teapot and two cups. (I couldn't help but look.) She offered Ani a cup and noisily slurped some tea.

"Well! Thanks a lot! See how you treat an old blind Indian woman. You won't even bring me some tea. You sit there and slurp right in front of me. Ani, Agnes is a real boksi, you know." Ruby stuck out her lower lip and pouted like a petulant five year old.

"But she's a good boksi, Ruby, a good witch," Ani said.

"Heeh!"

"I offered you something to drink, Ruby."

"You didn't offer me buttered tea."

"Do you want some?" Agnes asked.

"No. It's too late, now. This tears it. I'm going to go find Lynn." Ruby got up and walked toward me. When she reached the rhododendrons she stopped and felt the blossoms.

"Lynn, why do you always have your head in the bushes?"

"Ruby, Lynn is working," Ani said.

"That'll be the day. So, Ani, are you throwing me out? Is that what this all means? It's toward evening so I ought to be dead on the mountain in a few short hours."

Ruby hustled into the house to pack and Ani ran after her

pleading for her to settle down. I winked at Agnes and then shut my eyes. I thought of what Ani had said about four thousand languages, how difficult it is to penetrate a person's understanding if you don't speak their language. Then I realized that a culture grows out of the language spoken. Without language we are like complete strangers. But if one meditates or communes with someone, like I do with a crystal, there is a deeper connection. Silence, I decided, is certainly the language best spoken in these mountains. And I could use some of that silence from Ruby. She had just blustered out onto the adobe portal, her pack over her shoulder.

"It's okay, Ani, let her run away from the ceremony tomorrow. She won't miss anything," Agnes said casually as she gathered some flowers.

Ruby's head swiveled. "What ceremony? You never told me anything about a ceremony."

Ruby put down her pack, forgetting about it, and went to Agnes, her silvery eyes flashing with the reflected orange color of the sunset. She herself looked like an enraged dakini goddess, her hair frizzed in all directions. Ani took the pack into the house and returned to me as Agnes sat down with Ruby to talk about tomorrow and the ceremony. I wanted to listen, but Ani was searching my face for something.

"We need a universal language, Ani."

"Yes, we do. We shamans have one, don't we." Ani put her arm around my shoulders.

"Yes, the spirit language."

"Every place I have gone to work with my shaman sisters, even when we didn't speak the same language, we understood each other through the quest for spirit."

"Why is that, Ani?"

"Because the source of power is always the same." Ani placed her flat palms on the grass. "The source is always the Mother of all of us."

Leaving

Daughter, take these things—
this dress meant for cocktails
and dancing.
I want to be as
adorned as the seed
of an avocado, fleshless, slippery
when you try to hold it.
No good to anyone really.

Not that my dancing days are gone,
but I shall dance in my
own way, wearing my-
self, whatever that means—
an old blanket, something
woven by women, that shawl perhaps,
the one Susan made.

Or I shall wear beads and feathers I have
found and strung, strange amulets,
Spider Woman's lace, this
turquoise turtle
from the pueblo
that reminds me
how slow, oh so slowly
I grow

toward my own life.

—Elizabeth Herron

CHAPTER EIGHT

A GÚRAN

I awoke in the morning a few days later lying in a pool of sunlight. Someone had placed a beautiful delicate blue and yellow flower by my pillow. I picked it up by its tiny stem and tried to smile. I started to yell with pain, but my throat was so dry that no sound came out. I touched my chapped and peeling lips carefully with my fingers and winced. Ani sat down next to me and held up a small mirror in an ornate silver frame. Her turquoise silk blouse contrasted in a brilliant blaze of color against her dark skin. Her coral and silver necklace glinted in the early morning sun. Ani reached out to the patch of sunlight and gently moved her fingers around within it in a caressing gesture.

"House lights," she said. "She is our friend."

Her comment sounded so much like an old Indian friend of mine from years ago that I must have looked very startled. As I brought my memories back to present day, I realized Ani was staring at me. I winced again as I tried to smile unsuccessfully.

"Your body is trying to tell you something," Ani said as she held up the mirror so I could see my face.

I was shocked to notice that my lips were swollen bright

red. They were even cracked and bleeding from when I had tried to widen them into a smile.

"Oh, Ani, they are so sore."

"Why have you not tended to them?" Ani took a small bell and rang it softly beside my head.

"I was busy with other things, I guess." I looked at her sheepishly as I rolled up my mat and placed it against the adobe wall next to Agnes' and Ruby's mats.

"When you refuse to learn a lesson in this life, because you're too busy, or because you're afraid, or because you don't know how to stop doing a certain activity, the body takes over and begins to teach you."

"What does that have to do with chapped lips?"

"Chapped lips, colds, fevers, accidents—whatever you ask for, your body gives you."

"But I didn't ask for painful, dry lips."

"You didn't?"

"No, I certainly didn't."

Ani and I sat down at her wooden table as Didi prepared us buttered tea and tsampa.

"Could've fooled me," Ruby said, coming in from outside carrying several flowers and laying them on the table. "I was wondering when you were going to do something about that mouth of yours."

"Ruby, don't make fun of me. My lips hurt terribly."

"Then heal them, my daughter," Ani said very seriously.

"But how? It's so dry here," I said.

"You'll probably have to go home. I knew the altitude would be too much for a wasichu like you." Ruby giggled and sat down.

"I think you're both making too much of a deal out of my chapped lips. Ruby, your lips don't look so great either, you know."

"My lips aren't chapped. My lips are just fine. I take care of myself—unlike some people I know. You're just making fun of my wrinkles and I don't appreciate it."

As Ruby said this she held a tiny Herkimer crystal in the open palm of her hand. As the sunlight struck the prisms, rainbows flashed around the room. Then, all of a sudden, the crystal was about two inches above Ruby's hand, suspended in the air. We stared at it in disbelief.

"How did you do that?" I asked, astonished.

Ruby stood up and snatched the crystal out of the sunlight. "The same way you're going to heal your lips," she said, leaving the room with a toss of her head.

"Ani, was that a trick?"

"Everything is a trick in this dimension."

"I mean seriously!" I was getting exasperated.

"We are all part of a dream and the dream is part of us. We are the dream and that is quite a trick. Even to imagine the dream that is dreaming us is quite something."

"I know that on some level none of this exists." I made a sweeping gesture with my arms. "But my lips still hurt."

Ani propped up the mirror on the table in front of me. She rang her bell again and ordered me to stare at my own reflection.

"Who's lips are hurting?" she asked.

I stared into the mirror at my disgruntled image and swollen mouth. I looked a long time, asking myself who is hurting, who is hurting. The room went darker as I sat there. Clouds must have come into the valley and covered the sun. I felt like my head was made of pain, as if the rest of my body had disappeared. I was losing a sense of me, of self. I realized that I didn't know exactly who was hurting. Then I knew that no one was hurting. At the precise moment that I discovered this fact, my pain subsided and I looked up at the image of Ani's face behind me and let out a scream. Where Ani had been, a giant snow leopard now was. Her mouth was wide open in a furious snarl and she was bounding toward me. I leapt forward, overturning the table. The teacups flew into the air. Fortunately, I had grabbed the mirror in my terror. I spun around fully expecting to be mauled, holding my wooden chair up in front of me as a weapon.

Staring at me, mouths agape, stood Ani, Didi, Agnes, and Ruby. They were awestruck as I advanced with the raised chair, my other arm flailing at my imaginary foe.

"Get out of here! How dare you attack me like that. Where's the leopard? I saw her, she was coming right at my back," I screamed at them as I put out my right foot and stepped onto a round broken table leg that slipped out from under me. I landed in a heap with the now-splintered table and two chairs.

"We're leaving, we're leaving," Ruby yelled as she fled in a hurry.

"Fix that girl's lips before she tears the whole house apart," Agnes said, and quickly followed after her.

As I fell, I realized that I had made a terrible mistake. The whole upper part of my body was shaking as Ani helped me up from the rubble I had created.

"Ani, I am so sorry. I must tell you what happened. I thought I saw a . . ."

"I know what you saw, my daughter." Ani took my face in her hands. "I did not mean to frighten you. You worked much more quickly than I expected. You *saw* me. For an instant you *saw* me."

I stopped shivering and stared back at the old woman's face. Her eyes were unfamiliar and catlike. A cold realization inched up my body. I had heard about an ancient cult of jhagris from the Himalayas who could manifest themselves as the giant snow leopard.

"Yes, I am what they call a guran. This is an ability I learned from my power holder long ago. One day, perhaps, you will understand the need for this kind of power. Many think that this power is a trick, that this kind of power is evil or demonic. As an end in itself it is nothing, but as a means it provides many possibilities for good. You will see, and you will make a choice for yourself. Any manifestation of power takes enormous will and concentration and discipline. That is teaching. That, for now, is the most important thing of all. Remember, it is only part of a greater process that can be reached in a few different ways. This is a path of the warrior heart. It can only be reached with the courage of a leopard and the innocence of a lamb."

Without warning she changed again and became the Ani I knew. The odd glow that I thought I had seen around her now dissipated. Her eyes became sweet and gentle again. She giggled, more to herself than to me.

"What are you laughing at?" I asked as we picked up the table legs.

"Sometimes the leopard and the lamb inside of you get all mixed up." She held a table splinter up to the light as sawdust floated from it.

"What do you mean?"

"It looks like sometimes your leopard is innocent and your lamb has misguided courage."

I laughed with her, still not sure that this was all that funny. Suddenly I realized that my chapped lips were really better. As if reading my mind Ani reached a finger into an earthen pot and spread a strange-smelling ointment on my lips.

"This is made of calendula flowers from the valley and yak butter. New in no time," she said, pinching my arm and smiling as Ruby came back into the kitchen, her back plastered against the wall.

"Is it safe, is it safe? Don't hit me no more," she yelled.

"For God's sake, Ruby, I just thought I saw a leopard."

"Oh! Is that all?" Ruby's eyes glinted silvery for a moment. "How are your lips?"

"Actually, they're much better. Thank you for asking."

Ani replaced the chair and table legs in no time, smearing something like glue in the sockets.

As silly as Ruby can be, she can also be terrifying. She grabbed me by the arm, making me wince, and she then shoved me into a chair. She sat down next to me, looking at me out of the sides of her eyes. She is blind, but I could swear she was seeing me. She cocked her head like an owl.

"Today, you healed yourself," she said abruptly.

Ani sat across from me, making me nervous.

"When?"

"You moved into the center of your pain, and the pain fled," Ruby said.

"Yes, I guess it did."

"You did," Ani said.

"What do you mean?" I asked.

"You approached the edge of the dream and for a moment you stepped into a different dream, one you've never experienced before."

I stared at the two old women who looked suddenly much younger.

"We live in a dream. Dreams are like clouds dotting the sky. Sometimes with power we create a great wind and sometimes those clouds bump into each other. At that moment of collision something new becomes possible. You as a shamaness have the opportunity to confront the dream. At that moment you can change the agreements that you have with your reality and you can change reality. You had an agreement that your lips hurt and that Ani was an old woman. You moved into your pain and dispelled it. You confronted your agreement and denied it. By doing this you released energy and two dream worlds collided. You created a crack in time. For a moment you caught a glimpse of a different agreement, one not necessarily made by you. That's why you felt terrified and out of control. You saw Ani's agreement. That was a great moment of power for you, but, as usual, you became frightened and lost the moment. When the crystal levitated above my hand this morning, I told you you would heal your mouth in the same way. I meant it." Ruby pursed her lips and chuckled at my expression.

"You mean you changed your agreement with the crystal?" I asked.

"Not exactly. I changed my understanding with gravity. With the force of mother earth that holds us. But the change is created in the same way, and it comes from trust. A trust in what is true, the source. You climbed into the source and the dream was no longer necessary."

"Oh," I said, trying to understand the sense of something very essential and true welling up inside of me. Before I could stop myself, my eyes filled with tears. Seeing this, Ani stood up and put her arms around my trembling shoulders.

"Let's take Lynn outside to the rhododendrons. She always feels better with her head in the bushes," said Ruby.

We sat down under the bush. The sun filtering through the petals of the rhododendrons threw a crimson glow over our faces. It was true. I felt better there and I dried my tears. Ani reached into a small woven pouch tied to her skirt. She found some dried herbs and, crushing them, she spread them over a small puddle of water on the ground. The leaf fragments swirled and moved quite a while before settling into a configuration. Ani watched them intently, and then she closed her eyes. She was squatting on her heels and now she gently rocked back and forth.

"You have recently experienced a great sense of loss. Perhaps a family member has been near death. Is that correct?"

"Yes, it is true."

"But there is more, and most important of all—look at how

all the herbs clump in that one corner—you have an obsessive nature. Your life has great obsessions within it."

"Yes, I am passionate about life, wisdom, my friends . . ."

"You are also obsessive about your commitments once you make them. Like your commitment to the sisterhood and teaching, to writing your books. Obsessive! You're obsessive about animals, too. Beware, your sore lips are a warning. Your practice should be moderation," Ani said, finally opening her eyes.

"It's called, 'Lighten up, Lynn, or your lips will fall off.' " Ruby laughed to herself as she walked into the house.

"You mean my lips correspond to obsessiveness and a sense of loss?"

"That's just what I mean. I'm going to give you a tanka to meditate on. If you concentrate properly, it will help you."

Ani unrolled a canvas-like material and hung it on the wall by its red string on the top. She draped a purple curtain over the doorway and placed a pillow for me to sit on in front of the vividly painted tanka. Ani lit two candles corresponding to the edge of the hanging and placed white flowers beneath it after lighting some dried leaves for incense. They smoked quickly, filling the room with a cinnamon-like scent. After I was comfortably seated, Ani spoke from behind me in a soft, explicit voice.

"Witness this ancient Tibetan roll-picture. This tanka is in a mandala form. 'Mandala' is a word that comes from Sanskrit and it means 'circle.' It has a central point. The mandala is used to promote concentration and to help bring order out of chaos. The animals and figures used in this art depict transformation of the self through symbolism in its highest form. Deep meditation with the use of tankas can inspire you and cure illness."

"How can it cure illness?" I asked.

"By concentrating on forms wisely chosen by your teacher, you will move into a new state of being where your old illness can no longer exist. This may take a while, so let us begin."

"Us?" I asked.

"Yes. I will sit behind you and meditate as well. Often our needs are mirrored by each other," Ani said. Then, asking me to join her, we began reciting a mantra that she had taught me. After many repetitions she spoke quietly to me.

"The central picture shows the 'Selfless One,' Nairatmya.

She is dancing on a lotus with a flame surrounding her. The flames demonstrate the radiation of her power. She is accompanied by four goddesses who are separated by chalices on lotus leaves. Then there is another circle that shows the fields of the dead in eight segments. The number of the segments corresponds to an ancient Buddhist tradition that we are not learning here. What is important is to understand that our practices have mingled centuries ago. There is truth to be experienced here. Look closely at the fields of the dead in the next circle. For you must learn to die. Visit those fields of death in your meditation and examine your own dissolution. After this mantra we will begin."

She rang her bell and we began the mantra. After the mantra I fell into a deep and blissful meditation. I felt only a clear emptiness for a long time as I stared at Nairatmya. I had entered the mandala from the outer gates and slowly had progressed toward the center into the eight fields of death. It was there that I began to dissolve. Or else my thoughts frayed and disappeared and I seemed to disappear with them. I can only explain it by saying that I started to feel my body melt as if I were giving it away, not to someone, but to an element of trust. There was no need, finally, for a physical presence and I became lost in an embrace of the Selfless One. There was no sense of ego. I gave away my dreams and my dreaming. Hour after hour I unburdened myself of responsibility. The responsibility that I felt for my family, my friends, my animals, womankind. My earthly dreams seemed to slowly dismember. But for once it was not embodied in sadness or pain. The whole absurdity of my past was surrendered to Nairatmya, who moved about on the screen of my mind. She placed my heart, body, and soul in the vessels that separated the goddesses in her second ring of power and she merged with my essence. I observed in an explosion of light that only a realized being can take responsibility for another being. I knew that in my ignorance I could only present a mirror image to the world. It was the first step in learning how to die, Ani told me later. Then the tanka began to blur and I knew my meditation was finished. I rang my bell and recited another mantra with Ani. It was dawn and my lips no longer hurt.

Last Winter

A day the sun haloed
sheep against grey
winter grass. Trails
criss-crossing the hills and
fences what they know of home,

they turned backs to the wind,
that northern rustler who
kept me company driving
the flocked clouds south.

I was headed for the open
road and a dangerous
nostalgia filled me, knowing
this world takes us
far away, past sleep.

—Elizabeth Herron

CHAPTER NINE

THE SERPENT OF THE SKY

One morning before dawn, Ani awakened me very quietly and motioned for me to put my clothes on. She put some tsampa cakes and fruit in the basket she carried on her back and gave me a large bouquet of what she called white soul flowers to carry in mine. We put our white pashmina shawls (made from the softest neck hair in the Himalayas) over our heads as we set out down the path at a brisk walk. The sky was overcast. As often happens, cloudy days remind me of my childhood in the Northwest and I felt slightly removed from the surrounding village that slept under a blanket of fog. Even Ani seemed remote. I pulled on her sleeve, trying to keep up with her.

"Ani, where are we going?"

"We're catching the bus to Kathmandu," she said without turning around or slowing her pace.

After spending so much time in near isolation at Ani's house, the thought of going to a big, noisy city was horrific.

"Ani, do we have to?" I asked, dragging behind.

"Yes," was all she answered.

"But we'll be gone overnight. I didn't . . ."

"Maybe." Ani interrupted me sharply and I knew to close my mouth.

Usually any adventure was a good one, but not today. The wind was brisk and cool. I pulled my shawl around me against my encroaching depression and the relentless chill.

Hours later when we reached the bus stop, I was exhausted and thoroughly grumpy. We sat in the dust by the side of the road. Ani had decided not to speak to me and I sat drawing pictures of horses in the gray dirt. Finally, the bus, an old sputtering contraption with purple fringe hanging over the windshield and yellow paintings of the Garuda on the inside, came coughing and backfiring its way around the corner. Grinding to a slow halt, its doors opened and out poured a tour group of Bermuda shorts, sun glasses, cameras, raucous laughter— Koreans and back-slapping Southern-accented Americans.

"Hey, blondie, would you ask that old lady where the nearest bathroom is?" a red-faced man asked me as he pulled his polo shirt down over his protruding belly.

I pointed to the ditch by the side of the road, as Ani and I got on the bus. Several Nepali villagers joined us, replacing the tour group with bamboo cages of chickens and a small pig that squealed and snorted as it ran up and down the aisle. Ani and I sat side by side. I opened the window next to me. The warm air billowed over us, bringing the scent of rich tilled soil and spring flowers. The sun had come out and lifted my spirits. I looked at Ani and was going to apologize for my terrible mood but her eyes were closed.

Without opening her eyes, Ani said, "It's okay, Little Black Wolf Dancing."

I had not heard that name since a ceremony long ago in Manitoba. I was taken aback. How did she know that name? I stared at Ani, wondering why she had said that to me, but she had gone to sleep. Her body was swaying with the motion of the bus. For some reason, the way she had expressed Little Black Wolf Dancing put me on alert. Suddenly it dawned on me that something extraordinary was about to happen. When Agnes had told me about her baby daughter Little Black Wolf Dancing in one of our first ceremonies together, I had cried. Her tiny little girl had crawled out of the cabin and had been killed by sled dogs in the middle of the night. It had all happened so quickly, before Agnes and her husband could get to the little girl. Agnes gave me a dress that had been intended for her daughter's initiation. In that ceremony she took me as her daughter. It had marked a death for me as well, a death to life as I had known it. I thought for a while about Ani, and wondered if that was why she had spoken that name, to remind me of that experience so long ago.

I kept trying to argue with myself, to convince myself that we were probably going to Kathmandu for supplies. But why then was my whole body poised for some unknown threat? Ani was completely at ease. Her large coin earrings jingled on her ears. Her turquoise blouse and sari blew gently in the wind from the open window and her large creased hands lay folded and at peace in her lap. My body had become rigid with anxiety. As I was about to awaken Ani to ask her what was happening, she surprised me by reaching out with her right hand, gently gripping the back of my neck. In an instant my body-mind took over, like the muscles of my womb had taken over when I was giving birth. My lungs inflated and deflated in deep breaths that seemed to originate from my feet and circulated oxygen throughout my body. I must have lost consciousness then because I do not remember anything until I heard a loud snapping sound. Ani and I were no longer on the bus. I woke up as I was walking next to Ani. Had I experienced total amnesia? We were in a temple-like enclosure. I could feel the energy of the city in the ground under my feet.

A large stupa with the rounded womblike form at the top with the eyes of Buddha looking out over the courtyard was to our left. I felt the cervix-like form of the stupa in my body like a sacred mountain pressing into me. The small square or monastery was made out of ancient brick and smelled of smoke, cow dung, oil lamps, and rotting vegetables. Old men with red marks on their foreheads sat sleeping nearby, and several women in multicolored saris were lighting candles to a goddess place of worship inside a darkened room. Several pairs of shoes rested by the doorway and little puppies scampered in and out. They lapped at a puddle blackened with mud and oil from the lamps. Several greasy ducks joined them, and a few chickens pecked for seeds between the cracks in the bricks. Now and then a bell sounded as we walked through one damp passageway after another until we finally reached a chamber of separate rooms along a hallway made of dark stone slabs. Some of the doorways were inlaid with carved wood and painted blue and yellow in sacred designs. We pushed open a heavy carved wooden door with ornate dragons on the door handles.

The light inside the room was tinged with dark gold and pink. I could hear chanting voices droning from somewhere in the background. Occasionally a bell would sound. Hushed voices could be heard whispering from the shadowed corners, and sometimes a light would flicker in the darkness as if someone had lit a match. Gold, red, blue, and green painted hangings of various dakinis decorated the dimly lit walls. At one end of the squarish enclosure was a gilded statue of the goddess Tara, her arms gracefully snaking into a posture of bliss, her fingers curved in a delicate lotus-like configuration. I was vividly aware of the fact that I had lost several hours of time. I was walking through a red curtain with Ani and together we sat in a semicircle on cushions.

"Ani, where are we? Am I dreaming? Please answer me. Am I losing my mind?" My fingers were digging into her arm. I felt like I was on the cutting edge of sanity; one moment I was vividly clear and the next I felt cloudy and faint.

"You come to me with a true heart," said a female voice with a thick accent. I spun my face away from Ani and gasped. Sitting in front of us was a huge Nepali woman with a Buddha-like belly. I wondered how she could have entered the room so quickly and sat down without us seeing or hearing her. She was wearing a thin brocaded sari in gold and shades of red, blue, and green. Her round face was smiling and her eyes sparkled like black diamonds. Dozens of embroidered flags hung in rows over our heads. The room glittered with gold icons and mandalas painted on silk.

"You entered here through the veil of the dream because the way here must be kept secret. It is law. One day you will remember the dream and the way will become known to you."

I still don't know how a human being could be so enormous and yet be catlike, but she was. There was a feline quality to her movements and her expression.

"Who are you?" I managed to ask.

The two women burst into friendly laughter as they watched me try to cover my astonishment. I was at once repulsed and completely fascinated by the woman.

"They call me the Serpent of the Sky, because they don't know me."

The two women laughed again. This was a strange meeting without any of the usual ritualistic behavior. The woman was scanning me very carefully. It was almost as if she wanted me to relax so she could view me more deeply. Thinking this, I became more tense and they kidded and laughed at me.

"What does 'Serpent in the Sky' mean?" I asked.

"Who knows?" she replied as they giggled. Then getting abruptly serious, she said, "It means 'oneness with all life' and it symbolizes balance of the male and female principles. Here, I will show you something."

She picked up several stones and a small clear quartz crystal ball and handed them to me. I was so dumbfounded by the woman's almost American street-type humor and the obvious power that emanated from her being that I was stuttering words of thanks and I fumbled with the stones, dropping them. I looked across at the woman whose eyes had now turned to puffy slits with a tiny glint of light shining from within.

"Everything is in a mist for you. I will clear away the clouds. This is my first gift to you."

Ani reached into my basket for the white soul flowers and she placed them in front of me. I picked them up and gave them to the woman. She was very pleased and laid them across her lap, which sparkled gold and red in the candlelight. She closed her eyes and became very still. She picked up a bronze bell in her left hand and with a wooden stick began to make a haunting tone by circling the lip of the bell. Then she made odd hollow sounds with her voice as she held the bell up to her face.

"Hold the crystal ball to your third eye and hear me now." The woman was forceful with her words. I held the crystal to my third eye. I took a deep breath and tried to control the spinning feeling in my head, as if the sound was twisting my brain. I closed my eyes.

"There are many aspects of the Great Mother Goddess I call the Goddess Devi. We are each, one, and we are all of her aspects. I choose to call each aspect of her a face. Each of us as initiates lives one face perhaps for many lifetimes. You are not here to learn of truth as it relates only to the Nepali peoples.

You are here to learn of a truth that has been held by the power holders since the beginning of time. Before the Dravidians of India, before the Harappans and the Nayyars of Malabar, even before the Pon-Po of Tibet and Nepal, there was a knowledge whose face wants to speak to you. Her face has been shown in aspects by certain traditions. She has been misunderstood by most in their limited religious view. But she is the universe. She is the womb of all life and the source of energy for all that lives in the cosmos. Her arms enfold the young and the old and bring comfort to the sick. She is pure mind and yet she holds dominion over the material realm. She is the protector of those in harm's way, and she arouses passion in the lover as her breasts embody the sun and the moon in perfect balance. For each of the sacred luminous fibers—red, white, and black—she has corresponding eyes that match these sacred gunas, the threads of truth that create a connection between all material things like a spider web connects one corner of a temple to another. She is the one who embodies the wisdom that confronts you at this very moment. Look forth and see your guiding star, for I am Devi, the great mother as Tara, and I will protect you." The voice of the woman was quiet. Her words echoed throughout the chamber and then there was silence.

Still holding the crystal to my forehead, I opened my eyes. The room was filled with a white light so powerful that my eyes brimmed with tears but I could not close them. In place of the huge woman was a magnificent, radiant being sitting on a thousand-petaled lotus on a tranquil body of deep blue water. She was the white Tara, the goddess of wisdom and the protector of Nepal. Her face shone with profound radiance. She was so awesome that my heart was filled with joy. I felt a letting go inside of myself. Wave after wave of emotion pulsed through me as if a river were rushing through my arteries, clearing out all psychic debris. Without speaking, she communicated to me that I should place the sacred stones that the woman had given me on my chakra centers and let them collect the negative energy that had gathered there from my past lifetimes. She said that this teaching was about karma and a cleansing of my soul. She said that Ani would show me what to do.

"Keep your crystal ball always. She will connect you with your che-wa, your third soul. That is the light that you are seeing now. It is the light of consciousness. Che-wa is the light that shines from your own eyes. You will learn to control it in time. Your work here has begun." Without warning Tara vanished and the blackness of night filled the room. I heard shouts of alarm in Nepali and someone was shaking me by the shoulders.

"The crystal, where is the crystal?" I heard myself yelling. My arms were flailing around as I fell from the seat on the bus onto the floor. I heard the pig squealing and the bus brakes grind us to a halt.

"She will be fine," Ani said.

She had thrown me over her shoulder like a bag of rice. The next thing I knew I was face-down in the stream running beside the road. Ani used her foot to douse me good and then she helped me sit up. She used her shawl to dry off my hair and face. She waved to the bus so they would leave and then took my hands in hers and held them to her forehead. She whispered several words I did not understand and then peered hawklike into my eyes. I gasped and sputtered for several moments and then wiped the tears running down my cheeks.

"Here are the stones and your crystal. I will teach you how to use them, my daughter." She handed me a red brocade pouch.

"What happened, where are we—I—"

"I see the che-wa. Your third soul is stalking you, it will not be long. Say nothing, for Tara needs to rest within you. I know of your confusion. All is well and I am proud," Ani said, kissing my third eye, with big tears running down her face as she smudged my forehead with red pigment. "Come, we are not far from home." She helped me to stand.

I noticed that we were in another part of the valley, at a road crossing not far from Ani's village. The sun was setting, turning the great snowy peaks purple and pink. Every tree branch and stone glowed with crimson, as if the earth were on fire.

Grief

Reading poems
I question the grief

still in process moving through my belly,
the stiff contours of my throat, the shaking

that lives in back of my thighs, calves,
extreme targets of energy having rested

there for years burrowing in with my mind
saying do not feel, push down and now

nowhere to go except to feel
the slim connection still there, joy

remains behind and underneath
the grief as I allow grief to flow

out, acknowledging yes I have been
too long in pain.

—John Joseph Crimmins

CHAPTER TEN

BAHNI

The following day everyone let me sleep. Agnes, Ruby, and Didi had gone off to help herd sheep in one of the higher pastures. By noon Ani and I were sitting at her table eating some biscuits and drinking our inevitable buttered tea. The cooking room was cool and filled with the sweet aroma of barley.

"When you meditate today, I want you to invoke the image of Tara as you saw her. Become familiar with the feeling that you get when you bring her in."

"Do I hold the crystal to my third eye as I did before?"

"Yes, just as you did before."

I took the crystal out of its pouch and rolled it around in my hands. Its pink glow reflected onto the table.

"It's so beautiful," I said. "I have so much to learn."

"Yes, and this is a good beginning."

"Everything happens so quickly at times. I have always been the kind of person who lives many events in rapid succession and then I spend ages writing about them and catching up emotionally with what has happened to me."

"Ah," Ani said, squinting one eye, "you sound like a writer." She laughed and then her face relaxed and became serious. "These events do not happen to you. You are the event and you are the Goddess Tara. So when you try to understand a happening, remember that you are merely struggling to understand yourself. But I will leave the crystal teachings to a higher teacher who you will meet soon enough."

Before I could ask her who that was, there was a knock at the door. I put away my crystal as Ani let one of the young village girls come in to join us amid a tinkling of house bells over the door.

"Namaste, Lynn," the child said, her big brown eyes full of light. She handed me two brown eggs. One in each hand.

"This is Bahni," Ani said, leading the child over to me. "A few days ago, she asked me who you were and if you liked fresh eggs. I said that was your favorite breakfast."

"Bahni, thank you so much," I said, gently taking the eggs and placing them in a bowl. "Namaste, Bahni, I am so happy to meet you."

Bahni was about nine or ten years old. She had dark brown hair to her shoulders that frizzed around her beautiful oval face. Her eyes were turned up at the ends and her young mouth was full and almost always smiling. She wore a dark blue dress made out of cotton, an orange silk scarf, and was barefoot. Her small brown feet were callused and strong.

I wanted to give Bahni something in return, to let her know how grateful I was for the eggs and her friendship. She wore two dots of turquoise in her ears. Realizing that she had another pair of pierced holes, I took off my silver earrings and gave them to her. Her eyes opened wide with delight as she let the earrings rest in her open palm, the sunlight playing off their engraved flower designs. I took a wood-framed hand mirror that was lying on the shelf and held it up so Bahni could see herself. That's when I realized how shy she was. Her cheeks blushed bright red and she covered her eyes with her hands. We all laughed as she put the earrings on, very carefully, and grinned literally from ear to ear.

"You know, you and Bahni have one thing in common," Ani said.

"What's that?"

"You both have a great love of horses and animals."

"Ask Bahni if she'd like to come with me and I'll teach her a game that my father taught me when I was a little girl."

Ani translated for me. Bahni was gleeful and jumped up and down. I took her little hand and my carving knife. Bahni and I headed for the small lake to find a stand of stiff willow saplings. As we ran down the path, I stopped under a full-grown willow. I pointed to it and then indicated a smaller tree. Bahni took one of the willow leaves and pointed to the sky.

"Buddha," she said, holding her fingers to her mouth. "Words," she said carefully.

"Words of Buddha," I said, astonished that she knew some English, and even more astonished by the path her mind followed.

Bahni meant that the leaves rustling sounded like the words of Buddha. She seemed to understand what I was looking for. We walked around the lake to the west side. We walked through a group of several pine trees with Spanish moss trailing off the lower branches. I was delighted to find purple orchids blooming on the ends of several sal tree branches as we came into a clearing. I cut off two small, exquisitely perfect blossoms and put one behind my left ear and one behind Bahni's. She flounced around and did a pirouette, looking like a tiny Nepali princess, and then grabbed my hand. We ran down an almost invisible path to a large beige sandstone rock overhanging the lake. We scrambled up top and sat next to each other looking out over the water. We sat quietly for several minutes watching the afternoon wind make designs on the lake surface. Then Bahni pointed her small brown fingers toward the left.

"Baby Buddhas." She giggled as she pointed to the young willow saplings. Bahni stayed on the rock as I crawled down and began looking through the saplings for strong, straight trunks. I found four about the same length. They stood about four feet high. I cut them at the base with my knife and left a strand of my hair for the spirit of the willow trees. As I held them in a bunch I looked up at Bahni. She was standing on the boulder with her arms outstretched. On her left arm stood a little yellow bird. At first it hung on as if it were frightened, then feeling more sure of itself it hopped up and down her arm. I'd never seen a wild bird do anything like that. I noticed that it had a small piece missing from its tail feathers.

Finally, as Bahni giggled with joy, the bird fluttered to her shoulder. As Bahni turned her head it began to peck at her orchid. Eventually the orchid fell to the ground and scared the little bird into flight with a flurry of his tiny yellow wings. I stood staring at Bahni for several minutes. She stood still as a statue, her arms outstretched to the wind, her strange scarf flowing straight back. She was very childlike, but never childish. Bahni had the grace and imagination of an old soul. Her innocence was profound. I called to Bahni and asked her to come help me with the saplings. She picked up her orchid and placed it behind her ear and then scrambled down to join me. We stripped the branches, and after a few swift slices with my buck knife, we had four strong, fairly straight sticks that reached about shoulder height. Bahni looked at me curiously as we finished. I picked up two of the sticks—one in each hand, so they stood vertically touching the ground. Bahni took the other two sticks and did the same.

"Horse," I said, moving the sticks up and down like a horse's front legs. Then I whinnied like a horse and lifted the sticks into the air like a horse's front legs and reared back on my legs.

Bahni laughed out loud. She got the idea immediately and started trotting around as if she had four legs. She tossed her head as if she had a heavy mane, and tried to snort like the mountain ponies do. Then she stood, pawing with one stick leg, indicating for me to follow. I began to chase her, whinnying through the sal and pine forest. We galloped like two horses playing, kicking up our heels, and pretending to bite each other. We ran and ran, completely caught up in being horses. We were so possessed by the moment and our own enjoyment that we failed to see a grandmother carrying a huge basket of wheat on her back. We came blindly around some pine trees and dense undergrowth and fell headlong into the old woman, scattering us and the wheat all over the path. The three of us were so startled that we all ended up rolling around on the path, laughing hysterically in a mess of sticks and hay. We only became quiet when we saw the old grandmother roll to a stop at the foot of an elderly gentleman from the village. He stood there, mouth open, shaking his head. The toothless grin the old grandmother gave him was worth the afternoon. I quickly helped her up to her feet, and Bahni and I gathered all of her wheat into her basket. I was amazed at how heavy it was. With several namastes to the old gentleman, we giggled and grabbed our horse's legs and carried the wheat to the village. The old woman, wearing a blue and red sari and large gold earrings with a nose ring to match, was delighted and smiled broadly all the way home.

The next few days Bahni and I played horse together in between chores and my work with Ani. Bahni, more than a child, was like the little sister I had never had. We found a wonderful way to communicate with few words and mostly pictures and intuition. I looked forward to seeing her every day, and to the special eggs she brought me from her favorite hen.

The center clears. Knowing comes:
The body is not singular like a corpse,
but singular like a salt grain
still in the side of the mountain.

—Rumi
Tr. by John Moyne and Coleman Barks

CHAPTER ELEVEN
THE LORD
OF DEATH

Not long after daybreak, the sun's first rays lit up the valley. I had been sitting doing a simple visualization practice that Ani had taught me. As the sun illumined the dark-blue sky, I closed my eyes and felt the warmth and power of the rising sun within my own body. I also finished a long chant that Ani had given me. Although my body felt rejuvenated, my spirit knew that something was different. I stood and rolled up the small red Tibetan prayer rug that I had been sitting on. The brilliant sunlight made me squint and I pulled the printed dhaka shawl up around my chin. A blustering, cooler wind was blowing down over the craggy snow-capped peaks of Dorje Lapka.

I walked back down the path toward the cluster of village houses. I knew something was very wrong. As I turned a curve in the trail, I saw the small yellowish bird that Bahni had been playing with a few days before. I remembered how the bird, full of life and seeming fascination for Bahni, had landed on her arm. Now he lay dead on the path in front of me. I knew it was him, because there was a tiny nip out of his tail feathers. I picked him up carefully, but he was stiff and cold. I held him to my stomach and, closing my eyes and using a great force from my will, I sent his bird spirit up toward the light. I had often been told by Agnes that creatures need light and direction in the spirit world. They may have died suddenly and not even know that they are dead. It's important to send them on their way into the upper worlds with light. "It's light that they need," she had said. My heart was skipping beats. I started to run.

As I approached Bahni's house, I heard crying, a wailing sound of women's voices. Then I heard a soft male voice as I stood at the slightly open door. An old woman dressed in a white sari pulled aside a curtain and let me in. Her face was awash with tears. My eyes adjusted to the darkness of the small house. I blinked away the stinging sensation from all the incense smoke. A jhagri, a wiry old man with a face like corrugated leather, was doing something over Bahni's body. She lay still and at peace beneath many flowers that had been laid on her small body. Astonished, I looked at her aunt with tears in my eyes.

"They say that evil spirits took her soul in the night," Ani whispered in my ear. I had not seen Ani standing in the shadows. I couldn't believe that such a thing could have happened. Yesterday Bahni and I had been playing and having such a good time. I was horrified, and suddenly my whole being was overcome with sadness. I squatted down, my back against the adobe wall. I listened to the bells ringing and watched people file in and pay their respects. Several dogs came in and out and one curled up at my feet. The jhagri had been in quiet prayer for a while and now was dancing wildly around Bahni's body and beating his drum. He was wearing many bright feathers held to his head by a woven strap. His layers of white skirt and robes flared out as he twirled in a defiant ceremony. Two strips of bells on leather straps wound around his chest and shoulders.

"He is trying to find her soul in the other world, Lynn," Ani whispered.

"If he finds it, can he bring her back to life?"

"Yes. He is famous for this. But Bahni's soul has gone on. It was not evil spirits, it was the laws of karma that took her."

I turned to stare at Ani. "Shouldn't you tell them?" I asked between sobs.

"It is better left alone."

"How do you know that her soul was not stolen?"

"Because we know each other from another lifetime. I went looking for her earlier. I went to her guardians on the other side. They made it clear to me that she was already in the period of luminosity. It was there that I communed with her soul and I showed her the bardo of dharmata. She was too young to be with her guru. Her guru should be with her now, to help her passage in the bardos. We will watch," Ani said and turned back to the ceremony.

I was told later that at the moment of the girl's death the jhagri who was performing the ceremony had been called along with Lama Shingdo, the head lama of the village. Lama Shingdo was seated respectfully near the corpse with three other monks in dark robes. I couldn't tell whether the jhagri was successful in his actions or not. There was constant activity in the room. The family members were crying and consoling each other, their eyes filled with fright. The air hung gray and white with the haze of incense as the jhagri sliced the pungent tendrils of smoke with his purba. (The purba is a thunderbolt knife made out of carved wood and metal that is used to kill evil spirits.) He swirled and stabbed at the air over the body and finally collapsed in a heap of robes, beads, and feathers. Everyone in the room sighed. Then, more quietly, Lama Shingdo rose up from his seated position like a grandfather spirit of the mountains and extended his robed arms over Bahni's body. His long white beard, sunken eyes, and peaked cloth hat made him resemble Methuselah.

"Now Lama Shingdo will do a ceremony to extract the spirit from the body. I can tell that he knows she is already in luminosity, but he performs now for the family. Often a spirit clings to the body and what it knows. Lama Shingdo has been trained to perform a rite of passage to help the spirit go on and seek its destiny in the other world. He will act as her guide," Ani whispered into my ear.

Just then the lama leaned down and cut a few of Bahni's hairs from the top of her head at the crown chakra. I looked at Ani questioningly and in total shock.

"He is encouraging her spirit to fly."

I noticed that several boards had been placed on the floor in front of the praying monks. Long tablets had been placed on them. The lama went to them and began to examine the inscriptions very carefully.

"These are his astrology charts. He is trying to see how she should be buried."

A relative overcome with grief crossed the room to a pile of clothes and picked up the orange scarf that Bahni had been wearing the other day. I felt a surge of my own grief as I wiped my eyes. I felt stunned and alone, as if I were in the center of a mad cyclone.

"She must be very careful. Bahni's spirit could attach itself to her if she speaks."

The woman showed this scarf to the lama, but he told her to place it back on the pile as he shook his head.

"Why did she do that?" I asked.

"She was hoping to be given control of her spirit, Bahni's spirit. Lama Shingdo is trying to determine when the burial will take place, who can attend to her, and so forth," Ani said as she looked directly into my eyes and placed her arm around my shoulders.

I had become very withdrawn. I had been watching Bahni's older sister and her mother and father. Their grief was so profound that instead of wanting to comfort them, I felt that I was imposing my presence on them. There were at least sixty or seventy butter lamps placed near Bahni's body, along with bowls of water, sacrificial cakes, and other offerings. I looked from Bahni's body to a hanging mandala above her.

"That is a wheel-of-life," Ani said, watching me and following my gaze.

"Oh," I said. I could barely speak.

"See, those are the six spheres of existence," she said, indicating the painting where the hands and feet of the Lord of Death grasped them tightly. There was a flurry around the table in the next room. We could see through the light in the doorway as several monks and nuns got up from the table where they had been eating tsampa and tea.

Lama Shingdo said prayers over Bahni's body and then, with help from one of the monks, he moved it a few feet to the family altar in the corner of the room. He placed a dark cloth over the body, which was adjusted into a fetal position because in death we are reborn. The fetal position is representative of birth into this life and the spirit's birth into its next existence.

The lamas and monks, wearing simple woolen robes and carrying prayer beads, sat down in two lines facing each other. One monk raised a large conch shell to his lips. The pearlescent qualities of the shell caught the reflections of the firelight. It became illumined in pink-white light like a spiraling pearl. A long tone, coarse and primal, filled the room. For a moment everyone was silent and the tone echoed in my mind, cutting through my thoughts like the purba. The lamas and monks began to chant. Lama Shingdo was using another tablet with elongated pages.

"Lama Shingdo is using the Bardo Thodrol," Ani said, wiping her eyes.

"Is that similar to the Tibetan Book of the Dead?" I asked.

"Yes, that is what you people from the West call it."

Suddenly I was overcome with the heat from the lamps. I felt claustrophobic due to the cacophony of chanting, wailing, crying, and grief. Abruptly I stood up and headed for the door. Ani and the yellow dog followed me.

I was surprised to notice that the sun was near setting. It didn't seem possible that we had been in the house all that time. The brisk air off the snow-capped mountains was welcome. Ani grabbed my hand and led me up the steps to the roof of the house. Many of the villagers and people from the surrounding hills had gathered on the rooftop. The sisters and cousins of the family were busily preparing rice and tsampa in a big black pot. The old grandmother was sitting with a stick and wooden urn mixing the buttered yak tea. She looked up at us and winked at Ani as big tears rolled down her cheeks and made large puddles on her white sari. Ani took me to her and we nodded to each other. The old woman patted my cheeks and pulled on my ear lobe. She remembered the day in the forest. She knew that I had played with her great-granddaughter and had loved her. Ani and I sat down next to her, our backs against a wooden beam.

"The food is for the celebration after the burial. They will offer some rice to her spirit to help her on her journey home."

"Oh," I said. I was deep in my own inner thoughts. I felt closer to my own sense of mortality than ever. I was sinking into a deep depression.

"Ani, Bahni's death is so sad. How can they be singing and chanting downstairs and preparing food? I can't stand it." I started to cry.

"Black Wolf, you must learn to accept death." Ani was watching me and I saw great surprise in her expression. Ani dug around in the pocket of her skirt and brought out a small crystal. It glinted silver and clear in the palm of her hand as she held it up to me. I looked at it with dull eyes. I felt frightened and desperately alone.

"See into this crystal," Ani demanded. "It shines with clarity and life, does it not?"

"Yes, it does," I said, struggling with my tears. Then Ani gave it to the old woman churning tea, who nodded and put it in her pocket.

"Is that crystal any less alive now than it is in her pocket and you can no longer see it?"

"Well, it is no longer alive with the sunlight here," I said.

"But now the crystal reflects the darkness and the serenity of her pocket. The crystal is given a new chance to express itself. It moves on in its destiny and imprints new learning for its evolution. Bahni is doing the same. There were no more lessons for her here," Ani said.

"But what if that's not true? What if death is just death, the end?" I questioned.

"I suppose you've never healed someone with special energy. I suppose you've never met your allies and worked with spirits in other worlds, hmmm?" Ani was chewing on some tsampa and gave some to me with a nudge.

"Okay, I know there are many levels of existence, but right now I feel confused and horrified that I'll never see Bahni again. I can never seem to resolve the death of anything, whether it's a person, an animal, a relationship, or whatever."

"Your attachment is too great," Ani said.

"I know, but I can't help it," I replied.

The bedlam around us was becoming louder and the rooftop was very crowded with people, chickens, dogs, and a few small pigs.

"Come. We will go home and sleep for a while," Ani said, trying to pull me to my feet.

"But I must be near Bahni for the burial," I wailed.

"It will be a day from now," she said.

"How do you know?" I asked.

"I know. Now come, we have much to do."

I followed Ani back down the steps and out of the village to her house.

When we arrived at her house Ani quickly disappeared inside. Agnes was sitting on the portal inside a star configuration of rocks. She looked up at me from a state of deep contemplation. She patted the ground near her for me to sit.

"The rocks speak to me, my daughter. They say to me that you have lost a piece of yourself, like a shard cracks away from the mother pot."

I looked at Agnes. Her face was silhouetted against the streaks of pink and orange in the evening sky. Her eyes held the mystery of life. They watched me with kindness as I turned away. I wanted to tell her what had happened, but I couldn't find the words, nor the will to express them.

I had not seen Agnes for several days. The strength of her presence jolted me into a realization that sometimes we need to walk on divergent paths to come to a common fork in the trail. I looked over at her from where I sat in the dirt. Agnes smiled at me and turned to point to the small pond in front of us. It was to the right of the rhododendrons at the end of Ani's garden.

"What a fine mirror she is today."

"Yes, Agnes. She is beautiful," I said.

"Go look into her and tell me what you see."

I went over and knelt by the shimmering water that reflected crimson and orange from the sky.

"I see my reflection," I said, wiping away more tears.

"Do you look familiar?"

"I guess so—not really."

"It's a good thing that sky-mirror has a memory."

"How do you mean 'a memory'?"

"I mean that that sky-mirror remembers you or you wouldn't recognize yourself."

I touched the surface of the water with my finger. My reflection rippled and danced in the fiery glow.

"Some mirrors have a good memory and some don't, just like people. If a mirror remembers you, it has something for you to learn. If a mirror doesn't remember you, you better run and find one that does or you may be lost forever. Mirrors are all you have in this earth walk. If the mirrors forget you, you may as well find a good place to die."

Quickly I looked back at my face in the pond, seeing first Bahni and then myself.

"What does that face tell you?" Agnes asked.

"It tells me that I have been away from you for too long."

"Is that all?" Agnes waited for my reply.

In the water, I thought I could see an outline of an old Anasazi Indian pot with a piece missing at the rim. I imagined replacing the missing piece and then imagined the pot restored to its original wholeness. A gentle whooshing of air startled me. I looked up just in time to see a pebble arc toward the water where I had seen the clay pot. The pot fragmented into a hundred shimmering pieces as the stone hit the surface of the pond. For some reason, I felt shattered along with the pot. I couldn't imagine where the pebble had come from. I squinted and stared into the black shadows under the flowering rhododendron tree. Agnes said nothing. Then I saw movement in the shadows and the outline of Ruby's aquiline profile as a pinpoint of light caught the side of her face.

"Just like life, isn't it?" Ruby said.

"What do you mean?" I asked. I still could barely see Ruby.

"You think you've got it all together and, whoosh, out of the darkness comes a pebble and the reflection of totality is shattered."

"I guess so, but why . . ."

"Why is unimportant now. The fact is that life is a constant struggle toward wholeness," Ruby said, interrupting me.

"But the pot was whole. I replaced the missing piece."

"Never forget that this life, this dream that we are is a chimera, a reflection of what can be real and total. Keep on struggling with your lost reflections."

There was silence for several minutes. I felt slightly dizzy and kept blinking and took a few deep breaths. Agnes had seated herself next to me and had placed a pashmina shawl made of fine Himalayan goat hair around my shoulders.

"The pot you saw in the pond, does it remind you of anything?" Agnes asked.

I thought for a while. "For some reason it reminded me of Bahni," I said, starting to cry.

"In what way?" Ruby asked.

"It had great perfection like Bahni had. There was a quality of completion about her. She had such depth of spirit and color. The pot was like that. It was big and round and could hold a lot of life or water. Its color was subtle and yet perfectly executed."

"But there was a piece missing," Ruby responded.

"Yes."

"Did that piece have anything to do with her death?" Ruby wanted to know.

I trailed my finger in the water for a while, as a realization began to occur. "Her death was like me replacing the pot shard. Her death, for her, is another search. A search for her own perfection. Is that right?" I asked.

"Only you can know if that's right," Ruby said.

"Why only me?"

"Because you are speaking of your own reflection. In Bahni you are only seeing yourself and your own search for perfection and your own replaced shard. That is your own death."

I stared into the shadows, feeling very uneasy.

"There is also great emptiness within that pot," Agnes said. Agnes placed her hand at the back of my neck and swiveled my head. "Look into the water now and see."

I felt a subtle snap in my neck as I stared into the water that was now flaming red and purple from the sunset streaking the sky.

"What does empty mean, but being at ease," Agnes said. "Emptiness to be unoccupied and desireless. What you sensed in Bahni was her emptiness and purity of spirit. The pot is open and filled with the pure presence of the Great Spirit. It is motionless and serene. In Bahni you felt the pure presence within her. She was like a seed ready to be planted. All of what is in life is born from that kind of presence," Agnes said, as we looked at the renewed reflection of the pot in the water.

"You also are born of that presence," Ruby said, pointing up at the stars that were becoming visible above us. "The stars and this pond are born of that presence."

As I kept staring into the pond, I sensed a change in the pot's reflection.

"It's not empty anymore," I said.

I could see that the pot had become filled with something dark and rippling.

"What's it filled with?" I asked.

"What it is filled with doesn't matter," Ruby said. "Know that it is filled, and to become whole it must become empty."

I noticed that a piece of the pot was missing again, as I looked into the water. But this time a different piece.

"You cannot replace the shard until the pot is empty," Agnes said. "You see, all of our experience is like this. We fill up and become heavy. We learn and we take in emotions and circumstances and conditioning and we become cracked and imperfect, even chipped. We become full of illusion."

"Then what do I do?"

"Empty the pot," Ruby said.

"But how do I do that? It's only water and reflection."

"Only water and reflection?" Ruby questioned me.

"Reach into the water and empty the pot," Agnes said.

I tried to look into Agnes' eyes, but she gripped me firmly and wouldn't let me turn my head. A cold wind sang through the trees around the house. I felt strangely faint and yet filled with strength. I reached out my hand, expecting the pot's reflection to disintegrate as I touched the water. To my surprise, the reflection held solid. So I felt beneath the surface, realizing that there really was a pot sitting at the bottom. Carefully I placed my fingers around the curve of the pot, feeling its earthen quality and glazed smoothness.

"What you imagine is real," Agnes whispered in my ear.

With her words the inside of my mind burst open in a shower of light sparks and I felt a great force shoving me into the pond head-first and pulling me toward a giant ribbed tunnel at the bottom of the pond. I felt my body enter the water. It was icy-cold. I flailed around, trying to breathe, then my body went numb as I began to spin down into the labyrinth of a winding tunnel. I didn't question what was happening. I stopped struggling and went with whatever unknown force was pushing me. Maybe I was drowning. I didn't care. I plunged forward into infinite darkness that completely enveloped my consciousness. I began to see figures on the walls of the tunnel. Then they became animated and I realized that I was seeing people who I had known in my life. I was seeing painful experiences and situations that had occupied my heart and mind, experiences that had hurt me. I saw the tunnel going off in tendrils like arteries and veins. I saw those hurtful experiences clogging my blood vessels like gobs of cholesterol. I felt pain. The lack of emptiness was so excruciating that I somehow grabbed the clay pot and turned it upside down. I felt myself being turned upside down as if I were the pot. Out of my eyes, ears, nose, and mouth I saw words flowing in an endless stream. The words described in a steady pulse all of the experiences I had seen in my arteries and all of the people until nothing was left. I began to feel a hungriness; a voracious appetite was constricting my stomach and then that too left me.

The last thing I remember was Ruby's voice in my ear saying, "Only within the void does truth enter. Within emptiness, Lynn, you become pregnant with what you are searching for. You have died a little and your words have scattered in the endless currents of water. Bahni has journeyed into her own emptiness; like you she was looking for her true self. She has found what she was looking for."

The Wild Weeds

In the redwoods we find mosses
twigs, underfeathers
of hawks, tendrils
that move in the air
as if underwater

At sunset we climb the hill
where I gather you
with the darkness
your hair the rough fur
of some dream animal
your breath warm
as the earth all around us
the wild weeds

so we go home
finding stickers in our hair
our clothes, to bed turning
yarrow blossoms into stars
while barn owls sweep
the eaves above
our dreams

—Elizabeth Herron

CHAPTER TWELVE

DISMEMBERMENT OF MAYA

It was like being lost in a dark forest at night. I hung onto Ani's hand like a babe as we walked down toward the cluster of village houses below. As we rounded a corner on the path, I caught a whiff of sweet-smelling juniper smoke. We could see Bahni's rock house and could hear the beating of hand drums and the bleating of bone horns. A large funeral party consisting of all the villagers and hill people had gathered. Most of them had been holding a vigil all night.

"Lama Shingdo has decided to dismember the corpse and feed it to the vultures. It is good. She has lived a good life."

I stopped in my tracks.

"Ani, I can't do this. I can't watch such a thing. I cannot bear the reality of this kind of funeral." I sat down on the path and clutched my shawl around me and put it over the back of my head, sobbing.

"Reality does not disappear because of death. Life is eternal. In reality there is no death. What you will be watching is the dismemberment of maya, of the illusion, of the dream that we call life." Ani sat down next to me and wiped away my tears with the back of her fingers. Clouds were drifting over the sun as I looked up at the sky.

"What you fear is not the spectacle, but the truth that you are witnessing. It is your own truth, not Bahni's. She has already moved into luminosity. She has journeyed into what is real. You know you've lost the trail. You know in your heart"—Ani poked my chest—"what dies is only the unreal. Death proves that."

"Then what is left?" I felt frightened and lost.

"Bahni lost all of her endeavor when she died. All the things she had worked for, planned for. She is now empty of all that her ego was trying to accomplish. That's a hard thought." Ani squinted at me and twirled a coral bead on her necklace.

"Yes, I feel that emptiness, but it doesn't feel good like I thought it would. I'm not empty of my ego. It's like my ego is part of this."

"You see the wasted time. You sense what is really happening here."

"Please, help me understand this, Ani." I was in a dark well of despair.

"In this life—you are really dreaming. You may be dreaming of a beautiful heaven or the darkest hell, but a dream it is. When you awake into death you are left naked. You are naked of all that you have collected. You have lost all that you have aspired to do." Ani looked down towards the village as the drumming and chanting started again.

"Come. It is time." Ani pulled me to my feet. "You will see this. This is not for Bahni; it is really for you. Be strong. You know how to fight."

I stumbled down the trail after her, determined to hold myself together.

We joined the procession pouring down from the rooftop and out of Bahni's house. Then the funeral party emerged from the doorway amid a cloud of incense smoke.

"They often wait days for a burial, depending on how the spirit behaves. Bahni's was gone immediately, she did not linger, so they will have the funeral right away," Ani whispered in my ear.

The procession was led by several villagers beating hand drums and others blowing bone trumpets. Lama Shingdo followed behind them holding a long length of blue and white ribbon that was attached to the corpse. When I first saw Bahni I almost fell to my knees; they became so weak. Her corpse was covered in dark cloth and placed in a seated position in a large basket. The basket was being carried on the back of a villager. He was shrouded by a blue and red cloth. Bahni was followed by two men carrying large Kukri knives and axes. Then her brothers and sisters and parents followed. They were weeping and holding onto other members of the family. We walked slowly through the village. Several dogs were barking and chasing each other in and out of the procession, and chickens were squawking and flapping their wings to move out of the way.

We proceeded out of the small row of houses and down toward the river. The clouds were gone and it was a clear sunny day—the kind of day that would have delighted Bahni. A gentle breeze carried the scent of new grass and flowers up from the lower valley. I watched a butterfly as it flew around my head and landed on a yellow flower. I wondered if it knew that there was death nearby.

As we reached a hillock, a short distance from the river, all the women stopped. We were not permitted to go any further. We sat down on the sun-warmed earth as several rice cakes were passed around. Pieces of tsampa were lying on the path leading down to the river. They had been dropped carelessly by hungry followers. We continued our wailing and chanting.

The several men who had been leading the funeral sat down amidst the large boulders that skirted the river and continued chanting. With his hands Lama Shingdo smoothed the ground in a fairly large area. The man carrying the basket set it down in the center of the clearing. The boulders around them showed the marks of other funerals before this. Lama Shingdo and the others began the long ritual. Every once in a while a short blast on the horns would echo through the valley.

"They are calling the King of the Vultures. When he comes, the other vultures will follow. Bahni led a good life, so they will come soon," Ani said.

"What if they don't come?"

"It would mean that she had led a sinful life." She looked at me with no expression on her face.

"Would they bury her then?"

"Yes." Ani resumed chanting, as did I.

At least forty-five minutes passed. I watched the shadows pass over the mountains from the high clouds dotted about us like sheep. The men below were sharpening their knives on the smoother faces of the boulders. One man, who I think was Bahni's uncle, was sharpening the ax blade and testing it with his thumb. Occasionally the men would look up at the sky. Swiftly and with no ceremony, they tilted the basket over onto the ground. They uncovered Bahni's small naked body. Her eyes were opened and staring upwards. A man brought down his Kukri blade and cut off her ears. She was still wearing the small silver earrings I had given her. She had worn them the last afternoon we had talked.

"Her jewelry will be shared among the cutters," Ani whispered to me as she clasped my shaking hands.

"The journey of life is not separate from the end of the journey." Ani picked a yellow flower. "Look at this stem, Lynn. This is like Bahni's life." Ani held the soft flower to her cheek. "This flower is like her death; it is part of the stem and its growth. But the flower is a mystery, a great and joyful mystery."

With a single fast movement the uncle severed Bahni's head from her body with the ax. Its blade glinted with a flash of sunlight. Ani grabbed my shoulders.

"Now I pick the flower off the stem. I have isolated the mystery. That is all."

Then, with a matter-of-fact attitude, as if they were butchering a goat, the men cut off her arms and then her legs.

"Your mind is full of sky, infinite sky. Let there be sky and let the clouds blow away. You are full of learned things. Thoughts that make you stormy. Let there be blue sky."

One of the men had slit open her stomach and another was hacking up her legs into tiny pieces and laying them carefully on the rocks. Each piece was laid with reverence, like an offering on the altar.

"If you are afraid of death, you will not live your life. You will be immersed in your addictions to fears, to phantoms in the night."

Now the men, covered in blood and gore, were chopping up her shoulders and chest. They picked up the pieces carefully and placed them high on the boulders. Bahni was gone. Her body was completely dismembered and hunks of it dotted the warm smooth rocks like the ones she used to sit on to call the birds. Now a different kind of bird was being called. I remembered Agnes telling me about vulture medicine. "Vultures are the harbingers of life. They pick the slate clean and allow the spirit to be free of form. They are family birds with a great, wise soul," she had said. "Big medicine."

"Life is like a wave that rolls into shore. Then it floats back and disappears into the greater sea, until it peaks and comes up again with even greater strength. Life and death is like that," Ani whispered.

All this time the villagers were eating, chanting, and watching the sky. Then Ani elbowed me and pointed toward the mountains. Now the cutters had moved away from the boulders and had sat down to wait. In the distance was a black speck getting larger, and then thirty or forty choughs flocked the sky. To my surprise they did not attack the body pieces, but perched around the area. One or two swooped down to pick up a crumb of rice cake here and there. Soon after, a large ominous shadow floated over the gathering. Our heads swiveled around to watch a huge, silent lammergeier sail down from the north and make a pass over the circle of boulders. Several times he glided over us. He was awesome and he filled me with dread. He turned his head this way and that. His red eyes were framed by a black ruff beneath his golden head. This was the kind of vulture that Ani had warned me about. She told a story of one that had persistently brushed against her when she was on a precipitous mountain face as a young girl. These are the vultures that pick up the bones of their prey and drop them from great heights. They do this to expose the bone marrow, their favorite food. Several other lammergeiers soared near us, but they did not enter the circle either. They placed themselves on other boulders a short distance away and waited.

"They are waiting for the king," Ani said quietly.

A long time passed. I was afraid, now, that maybe the king vulture would not arrive. I could feel that others were becoming nervous, too. Then Ani pointed to the east with great excitement. A sigh of relief hung in the air. The griffins had at least an eight-foot wingspan. Their wings were decidedly square on the ends. They swooped down over the scene with awesome grace and dignity. Several times they perused the offerings and made it known to everyone present that the king and consorts had arrived. There were four of these massive birds. As befitting a king, he and his party did not immediately attack the display of meat. First they settled on the craggy cliffs above us. They lifted and adjusted their wings and also waited in respectful silence. I could tell which bird was king. He was in the middle and the others, very subtly, were observing him. He was sleek, powerful, and horrible in his mission. Everyone was quiet, expectantly waiting for his move.

Suddenly he sprung into the air and floated over the boulders for a moment. Then he did a marvelous thing. With a gesture of extraordinary grace and power he did a sort of death flight. He curled his wings in on himself and slowly and softly billowed down right onto the altar of sacrifice. With his expressionless pale eyes he hopped from one piece of meat to another. Was this meal fit for a king? Then, after testing several pieces, he finally landed on one and began to tear at it with his beak. Only then did the other vultures join in the feast. Now a flock of ravens also joined the party.

Slowly the funeral procession began to move to its feet. Quietly they started back toward the village.

"The birds will finish the ceremony," Ani said, as she patted me on the head and left me alone.

I watched Ani as she walked up the path, folding her wool shawl over her arm. I dried my tears and looked out over the stream and off toward the mountains. A large lammergeier had soared down to pick up a shin bone and then flew off to the south in high circles. The smell and taste of death was everywhere inside of me. Then a small gray-headed myna bird flew overhead. I noticed how its black wings became glazed with pink-gold from the slanting rays of sunlight. Bahni's funeral was less painful as her death became part of the mountains, birds, and nature. I heard the sounds of a human bone cracking against stone, and I watched the lammergeier as he dove behind a sharp cliff face and disappeared.

Out of nowhere a horse
brought us here where we taste love
until we don't exist again. This taste
is the wine we always mention.

    —Rumi
       Tr. by John Moyne and Coleman Barks

CHAPTER THIRTEEN

SUKU, WOMAN OF THE CHEPANG

Ani and I walked north on the trail out of the village of Buktimang and began to climb up toward the mountains that were obscured by haze. Ani had not explained to me where we were going. Two days before, when we had left her village, she had put enough supplies in our packs to last several days. The night before we had slept on the rooftop of friends of Ani's in a tiny village known as Pakatan. They had provided us with cotton mats and we had fallen asleep praying to our star sisters in the Pleiades which shone brilliantly above us.

Abruptly the trail took a curve up to the right and down through a stand of pine trees. Ani, who was walking ahead of me, pointed up to a tumbled pile of huge boulders that stood as high as any mountain I'd seen in the foothills of the Himalayas. We started to blaze our own path across lichen-covered granite shoals and fields of yellow daisies. Ani knew where she was going. After an hour of picking our way carefully through a forest of large-leaved trees—they looked almost like elephant or banana leaves—we came out on a clearing and sat together to rest and enjoy some dal, mashed soya beans, and tea. Ani nodded her head toward a particular collection of huge, rounded rocks.

"That's where we're going. There is someone I want you to meet."

"Someone lives in those boulders?"

I scanned the rocks for any sign of human life. A few rhesus monkeys scampered about, looking curious and afraid of us. As I sipped the hot tea that we had heated on my tiny Bunsen burner, I watched one of the monkeys high above us crawl into a crevice in the rocks. Then I realized that there were several holes, or what looked like the mouths of different caves, scattered along a ridge.

"Ani, are there cave dwellings up there?"

Ani nodded her head and continued to eat.

"Does anyone live in them?"

Ani nodded her head again and rolled her eyes. I looked back up at the ridge line of caves and gasped. Above the place where the monkeys had been, a wild-looking figure stood.

"Ani, look, over there." I was afraid to point.

Ani turned to look. Standing on a brown boulder, glinting in the misty sunlight from the pieces of flat mica embedded on its surface, was a woman. Her long gray hair stood out in a frenzied halo around her face. A nose ornament of what looked like bone accentuated her flat features. The light shone with a dark gleam off her high cheekbones. She held a bundle of what looked like the small green leaves from the sal trees around us. Carefully, she bent at the waist and laid them down. Standing again, she just looked at us. I was surprised to see that some of the leaves remained on her and then I realized that she was dressed in leaves and what looked like jute bags or material. Ani took out a wooden pestle from her pack and began to run it around the lip of the small bronze bowl that had held her rice. The bowl began to sing. As it reached the height of its toning, Ani held it out toward the woman in a wordless communication. The woman seemed to accept the offering, or she recognized Ani, because she picked up some leaves and began to beat on them in a rustle of primitive rhythm. Then the woman disappeared into a cave and Ani quickly gathered our things.

"It is time. We are welcome here," Ani said as we began to climb up the boulders.

I realized that we were following an almost imperceptible

trail, but a faint trail it was. My heart was pounding from the climb and excitement at meeting this strange woman. She had been standing farther away than I thought. As we reached a crest of rocks, I suddenly heard the plunging of creek water below. I looked across the bleak broken hills that were cracked into numerous ravines and fissures strewn with more boulders. The steep sides were impassable and shone raw white in the hazy light. I sat down on a boulder to catch my breath. It was covered with pieces of flint and tiny pebbles of jasper. A lone scraggly Himalayan cedar tree hung onto a flat mooring in a slate-filled crevice. A gust of warm wind brought a resinous odor that reminded me of Manitoba. Several monkeys huddled together on one of its bushy branches eating cedar nuts and dropping cedar cones down onto the ledge.

We continued around a precipitous cliff, placing our feet very carefully on the narrow ledge full of shale, and then we entered a forbidding dark, shadowy opening. The ground leveled out as we walked forward under an arch beneath the now-gloomy blackness of the high rocks. Slashes of light like bars made of fine dust accentuated the shadows as they illuminated the cracks between the masses of granite. I realized that we were in a village; several mud huts with thatched roofs were dotted around the area. As my eyes became accustomed to the gloom, I picked out the signs of life. There were a few simple baskets set near the entrance to a cave. There was evidence of a recent fire. Then I became aware of an acrid smell of something burning. We saw no one, but as Ani led me to a certain cave, I caught glimpses of strange-looking people off in the shadows. I had a sense that whoever they were, they did not like us very much. I kept close to Ani as we entered the black mouth of a low cave. I could see no light. Ani took my hands and placed them on the dry, smooth north wall.

"Feel with your fingers," she commanded.

I felt around and discovered what felt like several oblong shapes in relief from the rock.

"Here," I said.

"Remember the shapes," Ani told me as we went around a U-shaped corner and into a blast of firelight.

Several naked brown children ran out of the room and left us alone with the woman we had seen on the rocks. The woman spoke a strange language of greeting to Ani. We sat down, our backs against the cave wall. We sat on fragrant leaves. They looked like banana leaves. She smiled at Ani and ignored me. The woman only had a few front teeth. Her eyes were glazed over in an odd way. They held great power, but as if her attention had been focused inward for so long that she saw very little of the exterior world. As she spoke with Ani and laughed with her, I could see that her life was truly an interior one. Almost as if she were so removed from us that it was only her spirit talking. She seemed nearly transparent behind her dress of leaves and jute.

Ani turned to me and nodded. I held out a small wood carving that I had made at Ani's request. It was of a bird. Slowly the woman turned her eyes to look at me for the first time. Her gaze penetrated me like a beam of laser light. I tried to hold her eyes but I could not. They were too intense. Instead my eyes filled with tears and I quickly wiped them away. She took the carving in her long brown fingers, which were furrowed with lines like a vegetable field. She held it for a moment, her lids closing, and then for several minutes she held it up to her third eye. After a while she opened her eyes and looked at Ani, shaking her head. The woman spoke with a tinny, rasping-like voice. I understood nothing as they spoke her language. Finally the woman looked at me again. Her eyes held a softer light and I relaxed a little.

"She says you should know her as Suku, woman of the Chepang, that is all. She is of the Chepang people, and she wants to know if you are ready to hear what the soul of the sal tree has to say about your soul. She also wants to know what shape you felt as you entered the cave. That tells her about your journey here."

"I think I am ready. Yes, I am most eager. The shape was long, oblong," I said.

Ani spoke to Suku and then, adjusting her position as the fire spit up sparks from the burning branches, she began to translate directly to me.

"She says that there are demons near you, but that they are of your own birth. You have created them from your own doubt."

"Doubt of what?" I asked.

The woman held my carving again to her third eye.

"The doubt comes from your despair. You have been given

a difficult path, a lonely one. You have reached a fork in the trail. But you will take the correct path and you will slay the demons that confront you. Ani will teach you how."

The woman began to visibly shake. The leaves around her body began to shiver and rustle like a tropical storm blowing through palm trees. It frightened me and I looked wide-eyed at Ani. Ani shook her head and held her finger to her lips.

"The goddess shakes on her," Ani whispered.

The woman's eyes rolled back in her head as she lurched this way and that, her body seemingly given over to the more zestful animation of her tutelary spirit. She did not speak during this time. Her trance lasted for fifteen minutes or so and then she became very placid. She took a red blossom from the pine and flower garland around her neck and handed it to me. I smelled its sweet fragrance and held it in my lap.

"The goddesses say that you must marry," Ani translated as she raised her eyebrows. "Before a marriage on this plane can exist, you must marry your spirit husband. You are bun jhagri woman, you have the spirit. It comes through you with light, white light around your body, blue, too, and pink, but another spirit stalks you and it means to be your husband, your spirit husband. Any man who marries you must understand that first you marry Spirit Man. He balances your power and gives you strength." Ani paused for a moment as she spoke to the woman.

"She wants to know if you understand her." Ani's eyes had turned into straight black lines across her face.

"Yes, but how do I meet my spirit husband?"

"I will give you a stone. It is of my people, the Chepang. It will help your Spirit Man find you. There is a desert of blackness out here"—the woman held her arms out in a circular fashion—"and this stone will guide him to your light; it will guide him through the long darkness. He needs to see the light."

The woman reached around and moved her ox-skin drum and found a small basket. She took something out of it. Next she covered the object with ashes from the fire, then spit on it and chanted quietly, rocking back and forth as if she were holding a baby. Her swaying body cast an enormous phantom shadow onto the dark cave wall. I felt like we were in a forgotten earth womb outside and forgotten by relative time and space.

Suku, with her ferocious, wild appearance, held the grace, beauty, and sweetness of a great wise woman. Her movements were gentle and thoughtful, and her expressions revealed the careful wisdom of a sage. Her appearance of almost a wild animal had nothing to do with her elegant soul, which shone through her eyes in the way she looked at me. I wondered about her, how had she come to incarnate here, what lessons she had needed to learn. I was so fascinated by her cave dwelling and the sheer existence of her that I didn't realize that she was holding something out to me. Ani nudged me. Suku was holding out a small stone in the palm of her hand. She smiled her first smile at me.

"Thank you," I said, feeling the stone's smoothness. I studied its black and white lines, turning it over and over with my fingers. Then I held it to my third eye. It felt warm.

"Shall I do something special with it?"

"You need do nothing. Tonight we will call your Spirit Man in ceremony. We will drink a small bit of gittsa made from our sacred root. Your Spirit Man will come. We will have a marriage ceremony."

I stared at her and then at Ani. They both laughed at me.

"Ani, I don't take drugs. I've heard that this gittsa root is very poisonous."

"Settle down, Little Wolf, I will let no harm come to you. They take gittsa drink, we take gittsa only in the sacred dream. It is something like homeopathy. We only take the spirit or soul of the root. There is a sacred reason that the star sisters have brought you here. I know what you're afraid of. You're just afraid of getting married!"

"Ani, what is my Spirit Man exactly?" I asked, not laughing.

Ani shook her head and smiled. She thanked the woman in her language.

"Come, we'll go outside for a walk and go prepare ourselves at the river."

I bowed to the woman as I held my stone to my heart and left the small cave. All the way down the precipitous path to the river I was pulling on Ani's red sleeve.

"Ani, I can't do some primordial rite with poisonous drugs; this is absolutely crazy. Enough is enough, Ani. I'm going home," I finally said, as we sat on a rock in the sandy margins of the rushing creek water.

"That's fine. Go ahead and leave," Ani said as she busied herself with rice preparation and tea.

I looked around at the somber cliffs that lifted above me into infinity. I knew approximately how to get back up the trail, but then what? I realized that I needed a guide in these mountains. I had been foolishly talking so much that I didn't know where I was. I sighed and looked at Ani, who was giggling to herself.

"My daughter, you should know this better than anyone."

"What?"

Ani squatted on her heels as she washed her bowl with creek water.

"Always be receptive to the wilderness of the world."

"But I am. I love nature."

"That is not what I mean. The wilderness of the spirit is what I mean. Allow the mysterious and the strange to become part of your life. Be receptive to the non-ordinary mysteries of life. Many things that we humans need to learn cannot be taught in ordinary ways."

"I know this is a stupid question, but why not?" I asked.

"It is not a stupid question, especially because everyone asks it, not just you. You are not alone in your confusion." Ani sighed deeply and then went on. "Your people have denied the possibilities of magic, the light that is real even though it cannot be touched. The strange dimensions of life happen just as much as your scientific discoveries. In actuality your 'black hole' discoveries are the beginning of proof of the strange and magical dimensions of our existence. 'Strange' usually means only that it is something that occurs out of our frame of reference, out of our realm of experience. 'Strange magic' means beyond our understanding or the limits of our mind, something that is weird and bad. Mind is like this rice bowl, and rice is our knowledge. The rice is limited by the confines of this bowl. Be a magician, a jhagrini, and stay open to the mysteries. Let your wisdom reach beyond the limits of ordinary mind. Life, existence, is a mystery. Symbolically, your knowledge is not limited to a simple rice bowl, and that is the way it will always be. Instead of fighting for the rice bowl, fight to make beautiful rice. Yes?"

"Yes, Ani. I see what you mean." I took a deep breath and leaned back on the rocks. In moments I was fast asleep.

Hands

Hands take on
a certain prominence
in desert near stone.
They pulse
as if speaking say
work me bring me next to
hard rock where I can remember
something humans have learned
gathered and discarded
before this lifetime.

—John Joseph Crimmins

CHAPTER FOURTEEN

SPIRIT HUSBAND

My dreams had taken me back to my home in Los Angeles. I was sitting with my daughter on her bed, folding a pink satin comforter and talking about her college. Ani was gently shaking my shoulders to wake me. I jumped up and opened my eyes.

"Where am I?" I yelled as I heard the rushing water of the stream and sniffed the pungent odor of spruce sap. For a second I didn't recognize the face staring down at me with a grin. Ani's shield-like earrings tinkled against the large amber beads around her neck. Then I felt around me with my hands. Somehow I had gotten from the rock down onto the dry soft sand.

"Sorry," I said, sitting up and dusting my hands off.

"Are you ready to get married?" Ani asked me, a big smile on her face.

"I'm not even ready to get up let alone—how can we be doing this ceremony so quickly? I thought one had to prepare days, even years for such a ritual."

Ani sat down across from me. A half-moon began to peak over the craggy skyline above us that bristled with pinnacles and spires looming up out of deep purple gullies.

"You have been preparing your whole life for this ceremony."

"But isn't that true of anyone?"

"Yes, it's true in a sense. We are all on our own path. But for you in relation to Suku it is different."

"In what way?"

"There is a destiny to which you are giving birth. For this child of light to be born, the mother must be properly balanced and wedded in a sacred way to her spirit husband. It is law."

"Oh," I said, still not convinced.

"Let's meditate together. Sit comfortably and listen to the song of the river."

Ani seated herself a little behind me as she softly repeated a mantra and then very gently began to sound her brass chimes. Their tone pierced through the forest sounds and then mingled with them into nothing.

Again and again the chimes brought me up short and then dissipated my attention until finally I was relaxed and centered. Like the sounding of the chimes, my thoughts began to move in dialectical waves across my mind screen until there was silence. Finally there was only the gurgling of the river water.

As we prepared to go back to the village, Ani refused to answer any more questions I had about the demons that Suku had mentioned or about my Spirit Husband.

"All jhagrinis have a Spirit Husband who they are most intimate with. They mate with him and consult him on all matters," was all Ani said as she examined what she called my zee stone, the stone that Suku had given me.

"This is a very great gift," she said. "See, there are two holes in the ends so that you can run a string through it and wear it." Ani took out a thin waxed thread from her pack; ran it through the holes and tied it around my neck. The stone felt like agate and was oblong with black and white stripes in the center of it. It hung long on my neck as Ani held it up so I could see it in the moonlight.

"See, it has one eye," she said as I turned it and realized that the stripes came together at one point and formed an eye.

"Your Spirit Man will see through this eye and will enter the stone for the rest of your life. The agate comes from Tibet. It must be given to you and no one knows exactly where zee stones come from. They are very old. In Tibet they are also worn to prevent Akashra Rogue, or the Sky Disease."

"What is Sky Disease?"

"It is a kind of paralysis. Now, this zee stone is very sacred because it also has the power to call. Your Spirit Man will come to you tonight."

We started up the trail. After only a few minutes of almost vertical climbing, I stopped to catch my breath. I felt tired and slow. I looked up the path ahead and noticed that the pinnacles appeared statued with long flying buttresses along the jagged ridges of black granite. The mountain had the appearance of a giant cathedral in ruin, with jutting spires and dark cisterns of clay never to be opened. A fitting place for a marriage ceremony, I thought. I was fascinated by the zee stone and the proposed encounter with my Spirit Man, but I was lagging back as if everything was happening too fast. I was having trouble digesting it all. There was so much strangeness and the country was so wild that I seemed to be on overload. But I slowly trudged up the mountain, trying frantically to clear my senses, like sweeping cobwebs off the ceiling, and I readied myself for this mysterious matrimony.

Thankfully it was not cold as we reached the village. Men and women sat around in the dirt on the flat edges of what could be called a small village. The square was formed by five or six small mud houses made out of sod and bamboo and roofed with heavy grass thatch. At one end, just outside the entrance to Suku's cave, a small bamboo hut had been built with what looked like an altar inside. A straw mat provided the roof. Two young girls in jute with wild hair and kind eyes took our hands and led us into the cave. I had not heard of a jhagrini using a drum, or dhyagro. But Suku and another woman whom I assumed was a jhagrini were standing near the fire drumming loudly and chanting. Ani told me later that the dhyagro was made from the skin of a three-year-old deer, that there was a female and a male face to a dhyagro that was placed on a long carved handle. Suku addressed most of her singing to the female face. The female side is edged with white all around. The top half represents the mountains, the bottom the plains, and the dividing line is the river—all represent the divinity of the roads. The spirits of these are her helpers. Above these are stars dotted to represent the Milky Way, and in the center of the dhyagro are two crosses, one in yellow and one in red. The male side is painted with twenty white triangles, representing the balance of the male and female all along the edge. They also represent the mountains. In the center was an eight-pointed star.

The girls had us sit to one side, our backs to the cave wall. We sat on fragrant leaves set upon grass mats. We sat a long time watching Suku and the other woman, who was very old. They wore what appeared to be jute sacks covered with white clay and edged with sal leaves. The older woman had a white cloth tied around her forehead, and they both wore a strap of bells crisscrossed over their breasts. Only Suku wore a woven headband with dozens of peacock feathers, like a spiked antenna, sticking up above her head. Their eyes remained mostly closed as they danced around and around the fire, chanting and drumming constantly, their bare feet making a muffled staccato beat on the rock floor. I was fascinated by their use of the dhyagro. They held it up in front of them. The drum stick was bent in such a way that Suku would face the drum and strike it from behind, as did the other jhagrini. They would turn their drums from one face to the other, depending on whether they were speaking to a male or female spirit. I was captivated by their relationship with the drums. They would touch their foreheads to them as they played with heightened fury, speaking to them in loving tones. Next they would break into a wild series of twists and turns, brandishing their drums toward the four corners of the cave, and then the two women would put their heads together and chant.

"They are clearing the way for the spirits to come in. Start rubbing your zee stone now," Ani commanded. I rubbed the smooth stone and it became warmer between my fingers. The cave was becoming very hot inside and was filled with smoke from the fire and incense. After a long time of preparing the space for the spirits, an old woman came in carrying branches and laid them down by the fire. The other jhagrini sat down to rest and drink, and Suku took the branches and said prayers over them.

"Those are nettle branches to rid us of evil spirits," Ani whispered as Suku approached us and began to dust us, head and shoulders, with the branches. Then she threw the branches on the floor in front of the woman who had brought them, who immediately took a pine-needle broom and swept the nettles out of the cave.

"She uses a pine-needle broom to sweep out the pain and the evil," Ani said quietly.

"The house has been cleaned and fresh clay has been spread on the floors. And you have been cleaned," Suku said, looking at me. Ani translated for me.

"We will take gittsa and speak to the wisdom of the sal tree. We will call your Spirit Man. He is waiting for you. I have seen him. He is very beautiful. You will be happy."

For the first time I realized that there was an altar on the floor on the other side of the fire. On a large leaf, at least two feet long, were three-inch-high cone-shaped figures. There were at least thirty of the figures; each had a stick with a tree pod on the end near the top that looked like a parasol. Later, Ani told me all the details. In the center was a brass bowl of clarified butter with a wick burning. In that area was sandalwood incense, rice, a peeled hard-boiled egg, a few rupees, and a purba, or wooden dagger, with Kali carved into it and red cloth wrapped around it that had been soaked in blood. The figures made of cornmeal represented all the gods and goddesses. On each side sat two other bowls with red pigment and cornmeal.

The two women now sat in front of the altar throwing water and alcohol over the altar and offerings of cornmeal and rice. Then the woman helper entered the cave again, carrying what looked like a sal tree sapling. She dug a small hole and set the sapling into the ground. It stood at one end of the altar and they asked me to sit at the other end. I sat on sal leaves over a grass mat. Ani sat beside me, still with her back against the cave wall. Then the jhagrinis really began drumming. They cried out and danced fast around the fire and the altar. Suku stopped after some time and lifted to her lips a wooden bowl of what I assumed was gittsa and drank. She handed the gittsa to the other jhagrini, and then it was passed to Ani and me. Ani took the bowl and said a prayer over it. She took her left forefinger and put a drop first on her third eye, then on her tongue, and one over her heart. She handed me the bowl. I sniffed the blackish liquid. It smelled like sweet potatoes. Then, taking a brave breath, I dipped my finger into the liquid and placed a drop on my third eye, a bitter-tasting dab on my tongue, and a drop over my heart. When I gave the bowl back, Suku looked into my eyes for a moment. I could not read her expression. I was a little frightened and excited at the same time. The other jhagrini went over to the sapling and tied a string around its trunk after she had completely encircled the figures on the altar. Then she stretched the string across to me and she wrapped it around and around my right wrist. As the woman walked back and forth, I kept seeing her disappear into the smoke from the incense. Her body would fray into shreds that blended into the tendrils of smoke until they became one. I didn't think that I felt any effects from the gittsa, but my eyes did seem to be playing tricks on me. Suku now sat between the altar and the sapling. She had taken the bowl with the red pigment from the altar and the other bowl with the powdered cornmeal. I learned later that the Chepang raise maize to eat and they use it for their ceremonies. In other parts of Nepal they use rice or tsampa.

Suku washed the cave floor in front of the sapling with alcohol. Then she dipped into the cornmeal, as the other jhagrini played her drum and drew a big circle on the cleaned ground. The drawing of cornmeal became quite elaborate. Inside the circle Suku used the red pigment and drew a picture of a warrior holding a drum in his left hand. The other jhagrini was beginning to shake as she drummed. Every once in a while she would wail in a high tone and place her forehead to the drum and sob. Then she would hold the drum with great reverence, as if she were caressing a baby, and continue to sing. When the cornmeal painting was finished, the two jhagrinis rested and drank. They passed some water to us. We drank and Ani spoke to them.

"Everything is going very well. All of the spirits are pleased that you have come. They welcome you. Your Spirit Man is stalking you. You will begin to feel him near you," Ani translated.

Then Suku untied the zee stone from around my neck and tied it onto the string, between my wrist and the sal tree, very loosely so it hung down.

Next Suku and her partner began to drum and sing again. This time the singing was interspersed with cries and wailing. Suku placed my hands in a position of prayer, my fingers just below my chin. The fire began to leap and dance, as did the jhagrinis. Occasionally my zee stone would jerk up and down. Then Suku and the jhagrini sat down on either side of the tree. Suku took a folded piece of what looked like sheer cheesecloth. She dabbed it with gittsa and placed it over my head and face. It was long enough to touch the ground on either side and in the back. It covered my face, but I could easily see through it.

Ani translated Suku's instructions as the zee stone began to dance on its string. The two jhagrinis were now drumming, and then one at a time they would shake violently and then lie down next to the earth painting.

"Close your eyes, Black Wolf, and think of what you believe in. Hold the highest of your thoughts and let him come."

I shut my eyes. The interior of the cave had become like a sweat lodge. Perspiration was running in rivulets down my body. I could feel the zee stone spinning on the string. I wondered why it was moving all by itself, and then the motion and vibration of the string began to echo with the same spinning vibration within my body. I saw a glassy square of light in front of my mind's eye, like a polished window. As I scrutinized it, Ani whispered, "Go through the window." With that I burst suddenly through it and found myself spinning down a brilliantly lit tunnel for a long time until finally I came out on a high mountain plain. The fire, Suku, Ani, everyone was gone and I could no longer hear the ceremony or the drums. What looked like the Himalayas were all around me. Then I heard someone calling my name and the sound of thundering horse hooves on hard-packed dirt. A man riding a white stallion was galloping toward me. He was around my age and wore a black cloth helmet, peaked at the top and covering his ears down to his shoulders. He resembled a Tibetan lama in his clothing. His expression and eyes were fierce. The stallion had a very heavy mane and forelock. I expected them to stop as they reached me, but instead he bent down, grabbed me around the waist, and swung me up behind his saddle. I held onto him with all the strength I had. The horse moved with powerful, sure-footed strides. The man was strong and smelled of leather. I could feel the hardness of his muscles beneath my grip. We were going so fast. I closed my eyes and pressed my face into his back. Before long we reached an adobe cabin with a thatched roof sitting by a small lake. It was at the end of the valley. Here we stopped and dismounted. He was tall and well-built, I noticed, as he unsaddled his horse and set him free to graze. The stallion trotted off a few steps and reared, his ears flattened back on his chiseled head. Then he tossed his head and relaxed and began to nuzzle the patches of green grass, starting to eat. The man smiled first at the horse and then at me as he led me into the cabin. Inside he lit a butter lamp.

It was one large room with a bed, wooden table, two chairs, books, a fascinating collection of cymbals and drums, and a fireplace in one corner. It was cooler here and he made a fire. Then taking off his black hat, revealing thick dark hair to his shoulders, he joined me at the table. For the first time we sat and looked at each other. He was so beautiful to me, I must have gasped and stared at him. He laughed and then reached out for my hand.

"Welcome home," he said with great self-confidence and charm. "I have waited a long time for this meeting."

"As have I," I whispered, recognizing his voice and his dark eyes. "I remember you, don't I?" I asked, then laughed as I realized how stupid that sounded. "I mean, have we not met before? I know that I know you. And your horse, I know him too. His name is, is—" But I couldn't quite get it. "And your name is? I know that I know it. You have come to me in Los Angeles in my visions. Now I remember. You always scared me because you looked so fierce. Why didn't you talk to me? I could never understand what you wanted. Your face has tantalized me. What is your name?"

"You have used my name."

"I have?" I answered, looking at a gold statue of Shiva behind him.

"Yes, you have."

"Tell me, I don't know."

"The Gods call me Windhorse," he said, smiling at me through heavy lashes.

"I have used your name. Then it was you who gave it to me in my dreams. What does it mean?"

"In actuality, Windhorse means 'the exalted, buoyant state that one mounts and rides into the plain of enlightenment.' On many prayer flags printed in Tibet you will find a black horse in the center. When you hear the prayer flags in the wind you can hear the words of God being spoken. I am Windhorse and you are Windhorse Woman."

I stared at him, feeling an enormous sense of what I can only describe as relief. Tears brimmed in my eyes. I had been searching so long for some kind of indication of completeness at least on a physical level. If I were under the influence of gittsa, Suku, Ani, the ceremony, I didn't care. If I never saw Windhorse again, just having seen him once would change my life forever and give it great depth.

"You can see me any time you want. Just come to the valley," he said in his deep kind voice, as if he had read my thoughts.

"But how do I find the valley?" I asked.

"I will give you a key. You will understand soon enough. But first I want to show you something." He reached over to a shelf and picked up a marble statue and set it on the table between us. It stood about a foot high. "Do you know who this is?"

I looked at the Greek statue that appeared to be both male and female. "The statue looks androgynous."

"She is. She is neither a man nor a woman, though she is both and she nurtures both aspects of herself because she is complete within herself. She has learned to nurture her soul, which is her female side, and her spirit, which is her feminine side. All beings who come into my valley must understand this principle."

I nodded that I understood.

"She is the sacred androgynous Goddess."

"Yes."

"Are you afraid to die?" Windhorse asked me.

"I was, but not anymore."

He squeezed my hand. "That is good. Because to fall in love one must not be afraid to die."

"I'm not sure I understand."

"If you were afraid to die into me, then you could not love me. It would only be a foolish game. I showed you this statue because it represents a synergistic principle. Basically, being androgynous, her sum is greater than the parts of her." Windhorse smiled at me.

"I am not sure that I understand."

"This being has an ability that is more than the sum of her parts."

"What is that?" I laughed with him.

"She has the ability to truly love."

"And that's because he has nurtured the female and the male sides within herself to the point of perfection," I said.

"That's right. We understand each other. There is no need for conflict. If you were to dissect her, pull her apart, you could not find the love that is in her. It's in her soul and her spirit and it can never be found. It can only be felt as a functioning whole. Love can only happen through unity."

Windhorse leaned over and slowly kissed my lips and stroked my hair. I felt protected and safe.

"Come, let me show you something else."

He took my hand and led me outside to a sal tree. "This tree is like the world tree. You have climbed it to reach me. Your zee stone helped me to find you again." Windhorse reached up into the branches where my zee stone was hanging and, taking it, he gently tied it around my neck.

"You have always loved the trees. You love them because they help you hear the wind. Like prayer flags they also bring you the voice of God. In the leaves of the trees, you will always hear Windhorse calling you." Then out of his pocket, he took a tiny white horse carved out of agate and a small brass bell.

"From the bottom of my heart, take this magic horse and know I am with you. No matter how far or when, ring this little bell and my love will come to you." Then Windhorse took me into his arms and kissed me. "Don't you know that in every living thing I'll see you and remember," he said as he kissed my neck and held me close. Then slowly he backed away from me to arm's length.

I began to get dizzy. I frantically tried to keep my balance. I etched the image of the mountains around us into my memory, tears washing my cheeks. I gripped the horse and the bell as Windhorse turned into a body of pure white light. I watched, trying to keep my eyes open to remember his form, his light blinding me as he imploded into my being and suddenly I was back on the floor of the cave. I knew I was back and I didn't want to be there. I didn't open my eyes for a long time. Then I remembered the horse and the bell. I moved my fist and felt them inside. I opened my eyes to see Suku and Ani leaning over me, concerned expressions on their faces.

"We thought you were never coming back," Ani said, stroking my hair out of my face and eyes. I reached up and touched my zee stone.

"A day and a half has passed. It was much too long and we were worried. How do you feel?"

I just nodded my head as a signal I was okay. I felt a slight numbness and my eyes felt glazed over a bit. But I was so filled with an extraordinary sense of ecstatic contentment that I could only nod my head. I could not speak, or didn't want to. Finally I sat up and looked at the two jhagrini women. They sat across from me, smiling, as if they knew that I had lost a very special kind of virginity, my psychic virginity. The other jhagrini nodded and left before I could stop her and thank her.

"It is fine then," Ani translated for Suku.

"Now you know the blessings of a spirit husband. You need never be alone again. Now in your completeness, if you choose, you are ready to marry on this plane of existence."

For a long time we said nothing. I was deeply enjoying my sense of well-being. I realized that a spirit husband or wife awaits all my brothers and sisters, and now I can teach my apprentices how to meet them as well. This thought filled me with joy, because I now know the feeling of completion and ecstasy that this experience brings. Then I looked at Suku, who was sitting upright by the fire with her eyes closed, a faint smile on her lips. I reached over and picked up my dhaka shawl and placed it around Suku's thin shoulders. She opened her eyes slowly and smiled as she stroked the pink and white cotton. Then Suku looked down at her dress of jute and picked off one of the sal leaves. She held it briefly to her heart and then laid it gently in the palm of her hand as if it were a precious jewel. It looked smooth and shiny against the callused roughness of her fingers. Suku held it out to me, her dark face blending with the shadows on the cave walls as the fire sputtered.

"Sister," she said in Nepali as I took the leaf from her extended palm.

Animal

On the hump of rock, between
the little gulches that drop off
either side where the scat collects
I sit and look at it, pleased
to find this evidence of animal.
It seems a gift, my curiosity
a kind of rescue.
I look over the lake
                    (animal eyes, what would you see?)
listen to the wind
                    (animal ears, what would you hear?)

        I break open your scat
        to see what you eat. It smells of grass
        the alfalfa odor of baling and barns. No bones
        no small claw, tiny tooth or mat of fur.
        No seed or pit as in the bear shit south of here
        along the Tulomne. I break open another
        and another, finding only the green-brown
        of the lake inside each dark crust.
        Coming here tomorrow or tonight, you
        will find your scent released afresh
        from my search for your name.
        Whatever you are—raccoon? marmot?—you give me
        comfort in the solitude that
        scours me bare.

Now, in the late night house,
I nudge the logs into last heat
and undress by the fire, my skin suddenly
warm, alive in the quivering light.
For a moment I am something else
        in my nakedness, with
        ears and eyes and teeth
        of my own.

                              Squaw Valley 8/87
                              —Elizabeth Herron

CHAPTER FIFTEEN
LIFE IS A CIRCLE

"I'm sorry, I don't speak to strangers," Ruby said.

"Ruby, I have missed you so much. Please, give me a hug," I pleaded. Ruby got up from her chair on the portal and stomped into the house.

Ani and I had just returned from Chepang. After having morning tea in the village, we had walked up to the house where Agnes, Didi, and Ruby were sitting on the portal talking. Agnes gave me a big squeeze as Didi and Ani went into the kitchen laughing and chattering in Nepali.

Agnes was looking at the zee stone around my neck with a quizzical expression on her face. She raised her eyebrows and looked at me intently.

"Well, well," she said.

"Well, well, what?" Ruby questioned as she stormed back onto the portal and sat on the adobe ledge. "Nobody ever tells me anything. I thought we were family. Hmmph," she said.

"Ruby, we are family. I have lots to tell you, if you'd stop complaining and just listen. You never give me a chance to talk."

"Okay, talk," Ruby commanded loudly as she folded her arms over her chest. "You want to talk, then talk. I'm all ears."

I took off my backpack and sat down next to it on the red-mato-covered floor and tried to organize in my mind the extraordinary events of the past week. I was covered with a layer of dirt and grime. My clothes were so filthy, I was definitely thinking of tossing them away. My hair was hanging in matted ringlets, like that of a Hindu holy person, and I was so exhausted that I just looked at Ruby, completely speechless.

"Tsk, tsk," Ruby said, clicking her tongue.

I stared at Ruby in silence as she glared at me.

"See, I knew you'd keep it all to yourself. You're so selfish with your experiences. You never share them with anyone. I don't think it's fair. I've been good to you. In fact, I've taught you everything you know," Ruby exclaimed, taking her new red silk scarf and tying it over her head and under her chin with a big bow. She looked so comical I couldn't help but laugh.

"And now you're laughing at me. Well, the very idea!"

"The very idea indeed," Agnes said. "What do you mean you've taught Lynn everything she knows. I suppose I didn't teach my own apprentice anything, huh?"

"Well, you taught her some of the things I taught you; with the help of my Mother Rattle," Ruby said, fluffing out her red bow.

"I'm having a hard time expressing in words what has happened," I said. My thoughts were a jumble of images with Windhorse standing in the center. I didn't want to speak of him yet, or maybe I never would. My feelings about that experience were private, and they made me feel very fragile.

"That's just an excuse," Ruby said, looking very irritated.

I touched my zee stone in an effort to center myself.

"What's that?" Ruby asked.

"What's what?"

"That thing you have around your neck, of course."

I paused a moment in surprise. It was always a shock when Ruby seemed to be able to see as well as anyone. She must have sensed the energy flowing from the stone. I instinctively covered it with my fingers to protect it from Ruby's prying attitude.

"Humph. You got married while you were gone and you didn't even invite us. How could you? Now I'm really hurt."

Ruby got up from the ledge and began stomping around the portal.

I was having a hard time putting up with Ruby. I wanted to run away from her, but I didn't dare, so I began to cry instead.

"What is going on out here?" Ani demanded, as she came through the doorway and saw the tears of frustration in my eyes. Ani stood with her hands on her hips, surveying all of us as if we were recalcitrant children.

"Ruby is just having one of her tantrums," Agnes said, winking at me.

Ruby didn't say another word. She took off her red scarf and left it on the floor. It was a gift from Agnes. Then she left in a huff to go sit by the pond, her back to us.

I shook my head as Ani hugged me and went back inside. I wiped my eyes and looked at Agnes. We sat quietly for a long time listening to the house crows in the trees. Didi brought us some tea and biscuits. She tweaked my ear and smiled as she went back to join Ani.

"Come," Agnes said, pointing to Ruby. "Ruby has something to say to you. It's okay." She smiled as we carried our tea out to the pond.

I picked up Ruby's scarf and placed it around her shoulders as we sat down on either side of her. Ruby turned to look at me. I was stunned to see tears in her eyes. She covered my hand with hers. Her palm felt like warm leather.

"Look at the pond, my daughter."

I looked at the water and its placid, deep blue color. "It's beautiful," I said.

"Tell me what you see," Ruby asked.

"I see water that is quiet, like glass. There are images of trees, rhododendrons, and sky reflected on its surface."

Ruby gazed at the water then at me. "Yes. The water is clear and perceptive. You are becoming like the water. There is a new stillness. See that breeze there rippling on the surface of the pond?"

"Yes," I answered, watching the ripples of blue.

"The chaos of life moves over you like a wind. Now look at the bottom of the pond. What is happening to the plants down there?"

I watched the small water plants standing straight and quiet at the bottom. "They are quiet."

"Yes. You are becoming like a quiet pond. You reflect the chaos on the surface, but within you are silent. Your marriage is a good one. There is a new balance, and I am proud." Ruby picked a blade of grass that had a tiny drop of water on it. "This drop of water is like your medicine. It is like part of your mind that is wisdom. You are living your medicine. For a long time you have worked and struggled." Ruby placed the grass in the pond so that the drop of water was returned to its source. "When you first began your work with us, you moved into the greater sea of knowledge like this drop of water enters the mother pond. In your ceremonies and your meditations you became one with the pond. Now it is different." Ruby closed her eyes and gently brushed her knuckle across my zee stone.

"How is it different, Ruby?"

"Now the mother pond is becoming part of the drop of water."

I understood what Ruby was describing and again I was speechless. I nodded and smiled at her. Then, as if a dam had broken, I began to talk about Chepang and Suku. I drew little pictures in the edge of sand around the pond and even made a sand cone to show them what the deities on Suku's altar had looked like.

Finally, I began to speak of Windhorse. It felt good to talk about him.

"It's a beginning step toward unity," I said after I described the experience.

"Oh?" Agnes asked.

"That's what I felt."

"Only a first step?"

I looked at Agnes, trying to understand what she was asking of me.

"Yes."

"No," Agnes said, shaking her head. "All things are present within a single moment," she added.

"What do you mean?"

"I mean that your final step is contained within your first step. Life is a circle. The beginning is always the end."

The Hollow Mind

Christened with many names
forgotten in the last phase of the moon

buried in maps of private snowfields
on the road to awareness

the hollow mind
rattles

and shudders like a maidenhead
offering blood

the first time.

—John Joseph Crimmins

CHAPTER SIXTEEN
THE FACE OF GOD

Ani and I sat in a small tea-house just off the trail leading south out of the village of Buktimang. A small white puppy wiggled around a corner of the adobe building. He curled himself onto one of my feet and began to chew on my toes. I looked across the rickety wooden table at Ani, whose brown ears were filled with gold coins. A dhaka shawl made out of sewn layers of thin cotton in faded shades of pink and white was draped around her shoulders. She rested gently on her elbows as she examined a thin round metal object in her hand. An old red ribbon was tied to a loop in the top of the shiny disk. Chewing on her lip, she moved the disk in different directions so that it caught glimpses of sunlight and reflected them onto the thatched roof of the portal. At one point she caught the light in such a way that a rainbow splashed across her forehead and dipped into an earthen pot sitting on the red-mato-covered floor. When a young boy brought us tea, she covered the small shield with her hand and polished it on her sari skirt until he left. I had not seen it before.

"What is that, Ani?"

"Reflection means many things," she said, ignoring my question.

An unexpected clap of thunder jiggled the rafters as a warm rain began to fall outside. The spring raindrops made little puffs on the dusty untarred road.

"Reflection is a beautiful word, don't you think?" Ani looked at me over her teacup and, squinting one eye, she continued. "Reflection means thinking about things in the past or the future. To reflect does not necessarily mean to think about things that really exist. Reflection could also mean a mirroring, yes?"

"Yes," I said, as she uncovered the shiny disk again and held it up to the rays of sunlight slanting through the rain.

"This light comes from the sun. You cannot touch it. Does that mean it is not real?"

"No. Although some people say they need to be able to touch something to believe it is real." I wondered what she was getting at and was fascinated by the way she was playing with the light.

"Now look into the tea water. What do you see?"

I looked into the teacup as a pool of brilliant sunlight was reflected into it, illuminating even the dark bottom of the porcelain cup.

"I see the reflection of the sunlight."

"Yes. The sun and its reflected light are two quite different things, wouldn't you say?"

"I would."

"Which is real?"

"The sun is real and the glow of light in the tea water is only the reflection of the sun."

Holding up the shiny disk, Ani said, "This shield is a mirror for the sun. Now you see the sun reflected in its face and now you don't. Here, you try it." Ani handed me the disk.

It felt warm and smooth between my fingers. I examined it carefully. It was carefully handcrafted and it felt very old in its simplicity. It was a gold-silver color as if it were a mixture of metals. It had three circles with dots in the center in the three directions, and in the north was a copper loop with a strip of red cloth hanging from it. It was a slightly convex circle about 2½ inches across and thin but stable. I held it up and saw a somewhat distorted reflection of my face (with mottled red and yellow from the area in the background.) Then I held the small shield up to the remaining view of the sun through the mist of low rain clouds. A radiant reflection of sunlight bounced off the table. I played with the light for a while, directing it onto the red mato floor where three children giggled as they huddled together spying on us. Then the cloud layer became more dense over the dark hills and the sun was obscured from sight. My tiny mirror became a flat dense gold color, no longer as shiny. I kept turning the disk trying to find more sunlight.

"There, that's your problem. Do you see it?" Ani clapped her hands and laughed after sitting and watching me in silence.

"What—just because there's no more sunlight?"

"Let the sun go away. You are attached to the sunlight."

"But I enjoy the sunlight on the metal."

"But the sun has moved behind a cloud."

"Yes, I'm quite aware of that. Ani, what are you getting at?"

"I am just observing your discontent."

"I don't understand. I'm not discontented."

"You are dwelling on the past. You carry the past inside of you, right here." Ani tapped her head with her long forefinger. "Let the sun be gone, let it disappear."

"Okay." I placed the shield on the table between us.

Ani giggled at me. "You are still clinging to the sun. Like you do to Bahni." Ani took the shield and held it up to me. "Look into the mirror," Ani commanded.

I looked into the shield and saw my face.

"Has the reflection of your face changed this mirror one little bit?"

I thought for a while about atoms and molecules and then said, "No."

"Has the mirror changed or altered because it once reflected the sun or maybe even the face of God?"

"No, I don't think so."

"Give me your camera."

I handed Ani my camera. Deftly she set the flash and standing up she became a caricature of a photographer, kneeling down on the ground and twisting this way and that to catch the right angle and as much light as possible. She snapped several shots as a chicken fluttered noisily out of her way and the children jumped up and down shouting "Hallo, hallo," with their tiny brown palms reaching out for rupees.

"Ha! Ha!" Ani shushed to them in a commanding tone and they immediately quieted down. I gave them a few rupees and they disappeared behind the wall.

"The film in this camera is forever obsessed with the thought of you. Your face is imprinted on its memory forever. The film clings to your image. It is obsessed with you."

"I understand," I said, getting confused.

"This mirror reflects your image now," she said, holding the disk up so I could see myself. "But it is different from the film that also reflects your face. Do you understand why?"

I picked up the camera and the mirror. It never failed. Whenever one of my teachers asked me a direct question my mind would go absolutely blank. Ani took the metal mirror out of my hand.

"This mirror is not obsessed with the past like the film. The mirror reflects life, whatever is placed in front of it. When that reality shifts and changes, the mirror is left unchanged."

"I see."

Ani looked into the mirror and playfully arranged her hair. "The mirror sees a new reality. It sees me, but does that change me?"

"Does it change you? Yes, perhaps."

"That's right. Mirrors can change us greatly, because they enable us to see things that we may not have noticed. Like spinach caught between our teeth or the dark side of the soul." Ani winked at me. "But the mirror," Ani held the shield up between us like a sacred effigy, "never changes. The mirror is the sacred witness to everything that chooses to be reflected within its sphere. It has much to teach you."

"You are saying that I must learn to become a mirror."

"Yes, to become enlightened is to become like a mirror. If you have reflected the sun and then the sun sets, you can happily reflect the moon. We leak most of our power by our attachment to the images we reflect. We are like the film in your camera. If we become a famous jhagrini or healer in our life we become a jhagrini, not a woman living her medicine who happens to have developed the gifts of healing. It is the same for everyone—bankers, doctors, housewives. We never see who we are. We are obsessed with our own reflection."

"Is the mirror the source of reflection?" I asked.

"You are considering what is real, are you not?"

"Yes, I'm thinking about whether the mirror is a source."

"Only God is the source, and like the mirror we are mirror images of God," Ani said, tapping the metal disk with her forefinger.

"Then what is the mirror?"

"The mirror enables us to understand the nature of ourselves, of God. That is all. It is a sacred tool, a device for reflection, just as this physical body is a sacred tool or device for the process of evolvement into the higher realms. Our physical existence provides mirrors for learning. The mirror is part of the teaching."

The puppy that had been curled up asleep on my feet jumped up and started to wiggle and whine as he headed for a scraggly black mama dog with long teats skirting her underbelly. The shiny metal shield sat on the table. I looked into it and watched the dispersing rainclouds boil overhead as a hot wind filled the portal with the damp smell of spring rain.

A young woman came toward us. She was wearing a red printed sari made of cotton. She held her hands together in a prayerful sign of greeting.

"Namaste, namaste," she said, laying a lovely white rose in front of Ani as she knelt down and reverently touched Ani on the ankle. Quickly she was gone. Ani picked up the rose and smelled its fragrance.

"Perhaps this is meant for you," she said, giving the rose to me as we left the teahouse.

If you have a spirit, lose it,
loose it to return where with one word,
we came from. Now, thousands of words,
and we refuse to leave.

—Rumi
 Tr. by John Moyne and Coleman Barks

CHAPTER SEVENTEEN

AN APPOINTMENT WITH FEAR

The monastery where Devi lived was dark and cool inside. Ani had dropped me off at her monastery outside of Kathmandu while she went into town for material. There was a slight quality of dead sound, like in adobe dwellings in New Mexico and Arizona. Some of the floors felt like hard-packed ground edged with wood and in some places tile. The wood and adobe walls were clear of any decoration. A thick smell of incense tantalized my nostrils, but there was no visible smoke in the air. A gray wooden bench was set against the wall. I walked over to it and sat down, trying not to make a sound. I sat quietly for some time listening to the silence. Occasionally a board would creak in the ceiling as it expanded in the heat from the sun, startling me and making me jump.

At last a door opened at the end of the narrow corridor, flooding the area with a pie-shaped slice of radiant sunlight. A nun with dark clothing and a shawl over her head that hid her eyes motioned for me to follow. My curiosity piqued, I kept trying to catch a glimpse of the woman's face to no avail. She ushered me into an elegantly appointed room that I assumed was Devi's private quarters. There was an austerity to the furnishings. The tables and chairs were simple wood, but on them was silver, polished brass, and exquisite wall hangings in brocades and silk. Tibetan rugs or hangings were neatly placed over a daybed or couch along one side with soft purple and maroon pillows behind that and against the wall. I went over to look out a small window that was shoulder-high. The window was not made of glass and was not really clear. I reached up to touch it. I heard a noise behind me and spun around. As in our first meeting, Devi was seated in a low chair as if she had been there all the time. This disoriented me, and I just stood there stupidly staring at her.

"Sit down," she said, sweeping her hand in a very graceful gesture.

I sat down on the edge of a wooden straight-back chair. "Thank you," I said.

"Your eyes look like saucers. Am I that funny-looking?" she asked.

I was so fascinated by Devi that I must have been staring unblinkingly at her. She was huge in an odd way. Most of her weight was around her bottom area, making her look like an upside-down mushroom. Her upper arms were so long that they seemed like they should belong to someone else and her shoulders were quite narrow in comparison to the rest of her. This day she wore several layers of the simplest woven material. Her hair was salt-and-pepper gray, pulled back at the nape of her neck. She wore several bone and silver bracelets and a leather thong around her neck strung and knotted with huge round beads of amber and blue and white beads in varying sizes. Her face was young, like that of a girl, with high cheekbones and a full mouth. There was hardly a wrinkle and yet her hands were large, weathered, and veined with age like the creviced granite mountains that surrounded us. Devi was laughing at me. She reached over and took some butter-oil and lifted her skirt and began applying it to her long brown legs, which did not appear fat at all. I couldn't help myself. I kept staring at her, trying to squint a little so I wouldn't be so offensive.

"Here." She offered me some oil that smelled slightly like butter.

I put some on my hands, which had become very dry. "Thank you," I said.

"Are you afraid of me?"

"Yes," I said after I realized that not only did Devi frighten me, I was so completely terrified that I wanted to run to Kathmandu and catch the first plane home.

"Why?" Devi asked, turning her head slightly so that her eyes disappeared into shadow.

"Ah, I . . ." I really didn't know why I was so scared, but I could not even speak. Devi did not fit together like a real person. It was as if she were a collective idea put together by several people. Her head was huge on a skinny neck, tiny shoulders that melted into pendulous breasts, and an enormous stomach and hips attached to long, elegant, shapely legs, with ancient hands and feet, and a smooth young face with catlike animal eyes that alternated between soft and warm to icy-cold and predatory. For her size, she moved with extraordinarily graceful gestures.

"How can we talk, if you will not speak to me?" she asked in careful English, her voice soft, almost husky.

"Why is it that I keep thinking you are not real?"

Devi burst into sweet laughter, her whole body giggling in all directions. Her characteristic trait was gentleness, certainly to me. But I suspected something hidden from view, like cat claws retracted within a soft, furry paw. I could not shake that thought. Devi stopped laughing and wiped tears from her eyes with a white handkerchief ordinarily used by a man.

"Perhaps I am like this doll," she said, pulling a strange-looking doll out of one of her large pockets. She tossed it to me and I caught it by one leg. The doll was quite heavy, as if it were filled with sand, and it hung from my fingers in a rather grotesque fashion. I turned it around and sat it on my knee. I gasped when I looked at the face of the doll. It had a porcelain-like finish with features exactly like Devi. It was exquisitely designed and finished. It was a miniature fat doll that was an exact replica of Devi.

"Throw it up in the air," she said.

I threw the doll several times, and each time, no matter what I did, the doll landed in a seated and meditative position.

"We're going to have some fun." Devi winked at me. "We're going to see what makes me up. We're going to tear me apart. That should make you feel more comfortable, shouldn't it?" Devi looked at me and I could have sworn her eyes had turned yellow like those of a lion, but then she quickly looked down at her likeness, which she held now between her huge brown fingers. "Come, we'll sit together."

She moved us to two red cushions on a Tibetan floor rug and she threw the doll down between us. Again the doll fell on her head and miraculously righted herself to a tranquil, seated position. I was trying feverishly to quiet my pounding heart and relax. Devi had done nothing to me but be thoughtful. Then I realized that I had erected a barrier against her. I was getting a rush of excess feeling as a result of this emotional barrier and now, oddly, I felt a need to touch her on the hand or touch her being. I wanted to explode out of this sudden cage I had built around myself. As if reading my thoughts, Devi reached out and touched my shoulder, as if to steady me. Her eyes were deep, profound pools of reflected light. I took a slow breath and relaxed a little, the wall between us lowering but not disappearing.

Devi always sat in a precise posture of delicate tranquility, almost Buddha-like, but with her head tilted in a way that reminded me of the drawings of the Green Tara, and always the corners of her mouth were gently smiling. What a peaceful stance, I thought, as I looked at the doll and traced my fingers over the salt-and-pepper-colored hair sewn expertly into the doll's head.

"Like peaceful waters, so much is hidden beneath the surface," Devi said.

"Yes," I said, seeing a warrior's sword on the wall next to the door. I had not seen it until the sun glinted off the ornately carved handle and caught my attention.

Devi followed my eyes and raised her eyebrows. "The sword of a warrioress," she said. Her eyes narrowed momentarily into straight dark lines drawn across her face. "No matter what you do to this doll, she always lands like a cat in the right position."

I wondered why Devi chuckled to herself.

"Yes, she always sits in that tranquil position," I said.

"As you must in life. Whatever happens, whatever storms rage, this doll represents a likeness of what you need to accomplish. Tranquility and the position of inner meditation."

"Yes, I see."

"Let's see what makes her sit just like that," she said, lifting up the doll and giving her to me. "Feel her with your hands and see what you discover."

Soon I realized that the doll was filled with sand in its heavy bottom. I found a little door hinged on the back of the doll's head.

"Open it," she said.

As I did so a tiny bell fell out.

"You see, the head is empty, except for what?" she asked.

I examined the bell and found there was no ringer.

"It's a bell that can't ring," I said.

"Yes, it represents the sound of silence. Usually I make the head empty on the doll. But today I thought the bell was appropriate. Do you understand?"

"I think so. Thank you."

The same nun quietly knocked on the door and entered. She was still shrouded by a shawl so I could not see her face. She set down a tray of tea and two porcelain white cups in front of Devi and left.

We sipped tea silently for several minutes. Intermittently, Devi would look at me and smile.

"There are people who will try to hurt you. They come to you looking like flowers, smelling sweet. Never pick those flowers," Devi finally said.

"But how will I know?"

"These people want to use your power, your energy. They are looking for a line into you. You are very tight, but they look for a hint of fear, of weakness, and that's where they enter," she said, studying an area five or six inches away from my head.

"But how?"

"They might say, 'Be careful in the world, there are people who will try to hurt you.' "

I stared at her, feeling a sudden flash of fear.

"But you just said that."

"Yes, I did. Maybe I'm trying to kill you."

Were those claws I suspected going to finally appear, I wondered.

"Evil sorcerers want to have fun. They get bored. They find someone with light and power and they start applying pressure. Then you're in what they call a sorcerer's patch. They push your energy field until they find a weak spot and they pick up a line, one of your luminous fibers. They start pulling on it and then they find a way in. Eventually."

"You are fascinating me and I feel a power in what you say. There's truth to it. But there are different kinds of truth, aren't there?"

"Yes. There are truths you get lost in and truths that make you whole. Stick to the latter."

"So there are really sorcerers of darkness?" I asked.

"Oh, yes, but they must use your energy to function," Devi said, adjusting her large frame on the small cushion.

"I don't understand why they have to use my energy— you mean someone's energy?"

"Yes, a victim. Darkness in this context is only light that has not realized itself. Darkness is born from fear and greed. When you meet a black sorcerer, you meet an extraordinary ego, perhaps well disguised, but nevertheless an ego. That ego has become distorted because of some need, some fear that is so powerful that it produces a kind of greed that turns in on itself. It has a big mouth and destroys its own energy, it eats it and then needs others to fuel its battery. The patriarch, the male-oriented systems have had their chance. They really had a chance and they know they have blown it. A lot of the difficult energy you experience now is a death dance." Devi snaked her lovely arms and fingers through the air in a serpentine movement. "The current imbalance on the earth has a form and that form wants to survive like anything else. It is afraid of death. So now that energy is taking up a very bizarre strategy to try to win. But, nevertheless, the age of a sacred androgyny is preparing for birth."

"How do you see that happening?" I had forgotten my fear of this woman. Her words and way of speaking mesmerized me.

"Women as well as men are becoming the power holders in society. We are reinstating feminine consciousness. But this is a time to be extremely careful. Never think that power and freedom will be handed to you on a silver platter." Devi, with a sudden movement, was on her feet, swaying back and forth like a reed caught in the wind. Then she sank down next to me and blew a sound in my ear that resembled a northern windstorm. "Listen," she said, "the four winds are your allies. You ride the winds of time. You sweep through the centuries of your lives in the blink of an eye. We have all time and we have no time. Look at the t'anka across the room." She continued to sway gently and maneuver her arms in sylphlike motions. Her fingers appeared to be playing with the air currents from the open window.

As I stared at the image of the White Tara, Devi jumped in front of me and to one side. She moved so deftly, she did not make a sound. Then she stood like a statue staring into my eyes. Again her eye color seemed to shade into yellow. Carefully she moved her fingers in the air. Her movements were beautiful and purposeful.

"Look at the Tara and tell me what you see."

I stared at the Tara and began to blink as the image began to float up and out from the wall. Then it began to ripple as if it were made of water. Slowly it began to recede until only a pinpoint of light was visible. There was a tugging sensation in my midsection and behind my eyes. Then there was a blast of light that encompassed the room and I found myself lying on my back on the floor. Devi was gone and so was the t'anka. I sat up, holding the cushion to my belly, trying to keep from screaming. Moments later the door opened and Devi entered and stood before me.

"Stand," she said.

I wavered to my feet. Again Devi moved her arms in front of me in motions similar to T'ai Chi. I felt more tugging and then a general release of pressure. A smile returned to Devi's face and the intensity in the room dissipated. Devi sat down across from me and waited for me to speak.

"What just happened here?" I asked.

"I tricked you. I entered your energy field through your fear line. I literally grabbed it. I made you see what I wanted you to see. Because of your fear of me you gave away your power. I could use it in any way I wanted. That is what a sorcerer does. You think it's all mysterious, but it's nothing more than vicious manipulation. A sorcerer is a master of manipulation."

"But that was very powerful," I said.

"Yes, manipulating someone takes big smarts. And when sorcerers get results it builds their egos. But it makes enlightenment almost impossible for them."

"Why is that?"

"Because they mess with someone else's karmic field. That's not good."

"It's not good to indulge in fear, is it?"

"No, my daughter, it is not good. Fear leaves you as wide open as that field you walked through to get here."

The heart
never fits
the journey.
Always
one ends
first.

—Jack Gilbert

CHAPTER EIGHTEEN

A DARK SORCERESS

Four two-story brick houses sat at different levels and at odd angles from each other on the top of a mountain of terraced wheatfields. This was the home of the jhagrini Bina. A slow wind, warm and soft, blew across my face like fine sari silk. A rooster crowed intermittently and two puppies played tug-of-war in the dirt as a little girl wearing only a yellow blouse laughed delightedly. I could hear the sound of an old bus crammed full of Tibetans and Nepali hill people on the Arniko Highway, a narrow dirt road high above us. It is the only highway that stretches between Nepal and Tibet. They sang and laughed at the top of their lungs. It was five in the afternoon and sunlight brought a hazy glow to the edges of the deep-cut ravines and the dancing sal tree leaves surrounding the houses. A quiet had settled in under the transparent silvery light as the old men swapped stories and the women lazed on the portal wearing red, green, blue, and white saris. They all enjoyed the afternoon and the community in their wait to see the famous healer. Ani and I sat outside for a long time watching the pleasant afternoon turn into evening. Finally we were asked to come in.

I had begged Ani to take me to this woman. She was very famous as a Tamang healer and I was quite excited. Ani had been very reluctant, complaining about long, dusty bus rides into the remote mountains of Nepal, but finally I had convinced her. It had taken us two days to get here, so by the time we walked into Bina's small adobe room my heart was thumping. Our eyes quickly adjusted to the dim light. Bina asked us to sit down on the grass mats on the floor opposite her. The ambience of the room was dark and smelled rancid. There was a very different feeling from the light joviality outside. Bina did not speak English, so Ani began to translate.

"What is your problem, your disease?" Bina asked.

Bina was a slight woman in her thirties. She wore a gold nose ring, several strands of Tibetan turquoise, a red sari with a woven belt around her waist. A white bandanna was tied like an Apache headband around her forehead. Her eyes squinted at me as I handed her a pashmina shawl across her altar. The altar was a simple piece of oil paper with a dish of mustard oil burning and a twisted rope of herbal incense smoking. In an offering dish was tsampa, an egg, some coins, and a purba with the head of Kali engraved on its handle and what looked like blood on its blade. Lying next to her was an ox-skin drum with a carved snake handle. She took the shawl and placed it next to the drum. She looked at me with little expression.

"I have come to meet you and to honor your work. Namaste."

"Namaste," she said back to me, her hand beginning to stroke the shawl. "You have nothing you want to ask me? You have no ailments?" she asked.

"That's right," I said, trying to get comfortable on the mat.

Bina squinted at me some more and said, "Perhaps you don't know yourself very well."

"What do you mean?" I asked.

"A darkness has followed you here." Bina shook her head ominously.

"What kind of darkness?" My throat was suddenly tight.

"It is a darkness from across the seven seas; it was thrown on you in your homeland."

"What do you mean 'thrown' on me?"

"You have an enemy who is jealous of you. Have you not been feeling tired lately?"

"Yes, I guess so." I remembered how exhausted I was from traveling.

"It is only the beginning, my child." She picked up the shawl and caressed it.

"What are you talking about?" Now I was getting scared.

Ani would not look at me. She just kept translating and winking at Bina's three-year-old daughter, who had woken up and was lying on a cotton mat beside her. The child was stretching and coming in and out of sleep. "You have made yourself too visible in the world," Bina said, scanning my blond hair and American skirt and blouse. "You are a very fickle woman."

"I am?" I responded, surprised by her condescending tone. Bina was very unlike the other Nepali women I had met. But I knew she was a prominent healer, so I chalked up my discomfort in her presence to her attitude towards me.

"Have you had pains in your legs?" she asked.

"No."

"Are you sure?"

"Well, they have been muscle-sore from all the walking."

"You must understand that it is not me speaking. The Goddess Kali speaks through me. If you do not help me understand your problems, I cannot help you."

"But I didn't think I had any ailments."

"This darkness around you . . . have you had a difficult problem with someone in the past? It was very emotional. There was a misunderstanding. It did not need to happen. This person is trying to destroy you."

"Yes, there was someone, I guess."

"There will be a big trouble, very bad."

"A trouble?" I squeaked, feeling suddenly very achy and sore in my legs. Ani was beginning to shift her position as if she were very uncomfortable.

"It is very bad. First you will feel a general depression. That is the first stage, then there will be pus."

"Is there anything I can do to get rid of this trouble?" I was feeling short of breath and terrified. I thought of all the people across the seven seas. My mind was full of a jumble of nameless faces. And then I thought of Red Dog.

"It is very terrible. This person has been following you and is very relentless. But I can make him fall into a deep, dark hole for all eternity. He has been the source of all your problems. He is very ignorant and foolish to be tangling with someone who knows how."

"What can I do?" I was shaking.

"Bring me a black rooster tonight and I will heal you. I can get rid of this evil. It is best to be here at midnight."

"What will happen to me?"

"I will call another jhagrini—there needs to be at least two—and we will do a ceremony and do a blood sacrifice. We will sacrifice the rooster. I can free you of this pain and evil. Believe in me if you do not believe in anything else. Believe in Kali."

"But I don't believe in blood sacrifice. I can't do this."

"It is up to you, my child, but I fear for you."

Ani suddenly leaped up and literally grabbed me by the scruff of the neck as if I were a puppy. I yelled with surprise and pain. She dragged me outside and sat me down in the dirt.

"You stay here!"

She returned to Bina. I could hear an endless barrage of Tamang words. The two women were obviously having a huge row. It went on for fifteen minutes and Ani finally came out, grabbed my arm, and hustled me off up the road towards the bus. She looked furious and would not speak to me until we were headed back down the road on a blue and white bus with "TATA" in chrome letters on the front.

"Ani, I think you owe me an explanation. I'm so embarrassed!"

We had caught the last bus of the evening. Because most people of Nepal go to bed near sunset, we had most of the creaking, coughing vehicle to ourselves. I sat stiff and furious next to an open window that I was seriously thinking of jumping out of.

"You little fool," Ani hissed through her teeth.

"Thanks a lot, I love you, too," I scowled back at her.

Ani sat back in her seat and took a deep breath. She said nothing for several minutes. I couldn't help but watch her. Her whole face had turned black with rage or what looked like anger. But when tears brimmed over in her eyes and splashed down her cheeks, my own fury relaxed and I began to think about what had just occurred at Bina's. I was aware of my own fear. Fear that had been instilled in me by the healer. I thought about Ani's reaction of anger. There was no question that I was confused and scared by the strangeness of the entire incident.

"Why are you crying?" I asked very gently.

Ani looked at me for a long time saying nothing. Then with intent so strong that it nearly blew me out the window she asked, "What do you think we are doing here?"

I wasn't sure how to answer Ani.

"We're here to learn," I finally offered. I couldn't imagine how I had offended her.

"We are fighting a war, Black Wolf, and it is very tricky and it is very, very dangerous."

"What do you mean by 'war'?"

"We are in a war against ignorance and superstition."

Ani's intensity was bringing tears to my own eyes. I looked out at the moonlight reflecting on the terraced wheatfields and the mato-covered farmhouses, blinking furiously.

"I understand about ignorance, but I'm not sure what you mean about superstition," I said.

"You were just sitting on the quicksand of superstition. You were almost sucked down into something that could have destroyed you forever. I had no idea that you were so stupid." Ani reached out and touched my cheek.

"What did I do?"

"You didn't see what Bina was doing. You were convinced before we went in that she was above you. I tried to push you off the trail, but you were determined."

"Is that why you didn't want to go, all that stuff about dusty roads?"

"Yes."

"Why didn't you just tell me, for heaven's sake?"

Ani took a swig of water from her canteen and then offered me some. The water tasted good going down my tight, dry throat.

"You and I are on a special journey. Sometimes the signs are different. We have been given unusual tasks. Sometimes we don't always understand them. I didn't understand at first why you wanted to see Bina. Then I realized that you needed to learn something, something that I didn't know. So I kept my mouth shut. It came to me when I was watching the beautiful face of Bina's daughter."

"What came to you?" I was very confused.

"The innocence on her daughter's face was so true and sweet. She was in extraordinary contrast to her mother. Bina has lost innocence, but she is ignorant as well in her evil and her manifestation of it."

"What do you mean?"

"You needed a lesson in superstition and it would have been a hard one."

"How is that?"

"Because you're so stupid. You don't understand superstition and its extraordinary power. You are innocent like Bina's daughter, but you must not remain ignorant or you may find yourself in terrible trouble."

"I'm frightened, Ani. I don't understand all this."

"I'll bet you're scared. I'm glad you are. If you never learn another lesson, you better learn this one."

Ani got herself comfortable, tears still in her eyes. Every once in a while the bus driver glanced at us in his greasy, cracked mirror. He switched on the radio. Indian music crackled over the airways with a good amount of static.

"What is superstition to you?" she asked.

"I'm not sure, Ani. Something that is not true," I said, after thinking a long while.

"Your searching has become like a meditation. You, like anyone, cannot ask a question beyond your level. It is a law of nature. Your meditation, your being becomes elevated through your searching. I cannot stand in the way of that. You cannot manipulate the laws of nature beyond your level. People who have grasped higher laws are only people who have reached a level where they won't misuse that knowledge. Your Einstein searched and searched for truth and finally it came to him. If he would have misused that wisdom he could not have conceived of it. All great scientists agree on that. What lesser people do with that knowledge is something else. No one who has abilities and has grasped higher laws could ever hurt anyone."

"Do you think Bina meant to hurt me?" I was incredulous and filled with even more fear. Ani just looked away for several minutes.

"Tell me how you are feeling," Ani said as the bus lurched and groaned up a hill. I heard a mosquito whining near my ear. I took out some mosquito repellent and dabbed it on my arms and neck.

"I am feeling scared," I finally said.

"Scared of what?"

"I don't know. I guess of what Bina said to me, what she insinuated."

"Exactly."

"What do you mean?"

"I mean that that was her intent."

"To scare me?"

"Yes. Just that."

"But why? I thought she was a healer?"

"Oh, she is. She's a healer of disease that she creates."

"How could that be? People can't be that—stupid."

"Oh, really?" Ani took another swallow of water as we bounced through a small sleeping village. Several dogs barked once or twice as we passed.

"One of the biggest mistakes your people make in their lust for meaning is faulty judgment. They're either too skeptical and they miss important simple lessons or they're open and trusting. The world is full of false prophets and fakers. Just because someone is native does not mean that they are wise or are healers."

I giggled to myself, as I thought of all the trips running rampant in the U.S. "Some people have questioned my validity," I said, still feeling scared.

"That's a good sign. It's important for people to question. If you had done that today, you wouldn't be scared now. You gave away your power to Bina. I couldn't believe it."

"I didn't give my power to her."

"Yes, you did."

"How?"

"By buying into superstition. It is her way. It is the way of fear. A healer never inspires fear. A healer gives you light. A healer would never judge you or manipulate you or try to hurt you in any way. She saw your weakness immediately."

"How did she do that?"

"She saw that you were in awe of her. You have fear in you for some reason and she just grabbed those luminous fibers and began to tug on them. She pulled and pushed a little and you got scared. Once she tasted your fear she knew she had you. She knew you were from far away and of course you were tired from traveling. And everyone has people close to them that they have had arguments with. Particularly a pretty woman. She had you before you'd walked in. You didn't think of her as an equal."

"I didn't?"

"No. You thought she was better than you."

"That's true, in a way. I thought she knew things that I didn't. I thought she had special talents. I think you do as well."

"That's fine, but remember one thing: That doesn't make her or me any better. We are all reflections of that Great Spirit. We are mirrors, and some of us are more polished than others. Some of us reflect a little more light than others. That is all. Some of us have been around a few more times, have learned more. So what. In the end, what does it mean?"

"Not much, I suppose. But Ani, help me, my mind is not clear. Why am I scared?"

"I didn't know you were such a worrier."

"I'm not. She was just so intent on hurting me."

"What is frightening you really is your own superstition. People like Bina feed on superstition. This is a long conversation. I think we should try to sleep a bit. When we get to the village it will be dawn. We can have some tea and discuss this then," Ani said as she rolled up her shawl, and placing it in the hollow of her neck against the high-backed seat, she was instantly asleep. Her large earrings swayed back and forth with the motion of the bus. I fidgeted around trying to get comfortable. The heat was oppressive. Bugs flew in and out of the window and my back ached. I was hungry. Thoughts of Bina filtered through, try as I did to forget about her. I was immersed in a dark hole filled with grotesque monsters of my own making.

When we got off the bus it was morning and several people of the village were waiting for it. We nodded a few namastes and went to a small teahouse. Ani was rested, as if she had slept a full night on her own cotton mattress. We sat down at a square wooden table.

"Well, did you have a good sleep?" Ani asked with a little twinkle in her eyes.

"Not exactly. It wasn't the bus as much as my own thoughts," I admitted as I poured some milk into the tea that the young girl had brought to us. Ani made no comment. She just looked at me over her steaming tea.

"I was afraid of that," she said.

"Afraid of what?"

" 'Afraid' is not the right word. Actually, I hoped that you would wrestle with your thoughts."

"How come?"

"I really want you to learn this lesson. It is an important one."

"Okay, Ani. I'm all yours." I looked around at the tiny teahouse. The floor was spread with red earth mato and the windowsills were painted blue. There were only three other small tables in the room. Two brown and white dogs lay asleep in one corner. There was a musty earth smell in the air as if the house were very old. My eyes settled back on Ani, who had become very serious.

"We were speaking of superstition," she said.

"Yes,"

"First of all, superstition is an external term. So when I asked you 'What is superstition?' I was asking an external question."

"I understand."

"Feelings or experience is subjective. A person's superstitions are thought to be valid, because there may have been an instance where that person has felt something that has led to an external experience. Superstition is what is seen by deeper levels of mind, like a warning. This warning then leads to something happening."

"So we went to see Bina. She told me that she saw something evil and she warned me. If things had gone her way, the happening would have been the ceremony. Is that right?"

"Yes, and probably she would have told you other imaginings and so-called valid visions to manipulate you."

"Why do you think she was trying to manipulate me?"

"Because she was not trying to heal you or honor you, she was instilling you with fear. That is manipulation. She wanted you for something. My guess is money. You would have paid her anything for her help, right?"

"Right."

"So there you are."

"She did scare me."

"Of course. She is very good with the black arts."

"I still don't understand why you think she was so dark."

"Remember what I said?"

"What?"

"People who have grasped higher laws cannot misuse that knowledge. They couldn't conceive of it. It is a law of nature. If she were true, she could not, nor would not, dream of hurting or scaring you."

"Oh," I said, nodding in remembrance of our previous conversation. "Do you think she could see into the future?"

"If she could at all, which I doubt, she would not have the ability to sort out truth from fiction. She would not be able to identify actual warnings or indications."

"What makes a person want to hurt someone like that?" I was beginning to really understand what Ani was getting at.

"That sort of person is stimulated by greed, fear, poverty, or some deep unfulfilled need."

"That makes them want to manipulate others?"

"Yes. Those who want to externally control others are acting from a place of a deep lack of confidence and insecurity. It comes from a deep dependence that they don't want to admit to. So they give that dependence a different image by spreading it onto others." Ani stopped talking and looked at me with her head slightly tipped to one side. "You can only give to others what you have in overabundance yourself," she went on. "If Bina spreads fear, then she has an overabundance of fear within herself. If she is dependent, then she wants others dependent on her. Those who spread weakness are weak inside. It's a law of nature. You cannot stop the flow of what is inside. They have to spread what is inside of them."

"That goes for clarity, truth, and good things too, doesn't it?

"Yes." Ani nodded her head from side to side and crunched on a biscuit that had been brought up to the table. "Even if a person is not actually communicating, if a person is full of greed or fear, it will surround people near them. Say I'm full of fear, but I don't actually say that. I try to cover it up. One day your psychic immunity will be at a low ebb. What I have emitted you will eat. And you will be surrounded by fear and eating fear."

As we walked through the small village and up to Ani's house we said nothing. I understood what Ani had been saying. I was stunned into silence, silence that I was still so dumb.

All horse cultures
And the horse in dreams!
If I could speak of their manes hanging like metals
Hoofs tapping the rocks
And that wild look straight ahead in a fertile valley
  the sun

—Philip Lamantia

CHAPTER NINETEEN

DEATH OF A BLACK MAGICIAN

The next morning I took a walk with Agnes and Ruby. The sunlight reflected golden and white off Dorje Lapka and Phurbi Chyapu. It was so unusually clear that I felt I could reach out and touch their craggy spires. We hiked up to the top of a high hill. We could see a great distance to the south over Panchkhal Valley and the terraced wheatfields. We sat down on three flat stones, our backs to each other, each of us looking in a different direction. No matter how spectacular the view I couldn't escape the feeling of dread deep in my stomach. Horrible images kept floating across my mind until finally I had to say something.

"I told you both about my meeting with Bina. I also told you all the things that Ani said to me about superstition and sorcery. Did you agree with her?"

"Oh, yes. And that lesson is a very, very important one," Agnes answered.

"People who have some power and perhaps some charisma can get stuck in the Southwest on the medicine wheel. They get stuck there for all the reasons Ani explained, because of greed and fear," Ruby said.

"Fear is the worst part," I said.

"Yes. They spread their own fear to everyone around them. But the worst part is something else," Agnes said.

"What's that?"

"The worst part has to do with what makes the real difference between a medicine person or shaman and a sorcerer. A shaman healer has the courage to confront her own demons, her fears, the weaker aspects of her nature, and learn from them. She, to perfect her art, must go deeply into the open wound of her life and heal the difficulties of her personal existence. Then and only then can she begin to work with others."

"What does a sorcerer do?"

"A sorcerer gets hung up on power and stays in that tiny circle. He lives off the energy of others with tricks and sabotage. And never does he evolve."

"How do you mean 'sabotage'?"

Agnes turned around to face me by sitting down on the ground with her back against the stone. She was wearing a green silk blouse and the silver earring that Ani and Didi had given her. With her gray hair braided back and her dark skin deeply tanned, she could easily have been Tibetan.

"Sorcerers sabotage their own process of enlightenment by always dwelling on negative issues."

"But I don't understand how negativity can sabotage a person." I slid down off the rock and sat in front of Agnes. Ruby had laid back on the stone and appeared to be sleeping.

"Remember what Ani said about your experience being all that you have?"

"Yes, I remember."

"She also said that after death you join into the greater sea of experience."

"Yes, but I still don't . . ."

"There are vast levels in the spirit world," Agnes said, ignoring my confusion.

"Meaning?"

"Meaning that if you are a positive person with creative thoughts that you will naturally gravitate toward a very high spirit level of vibration after death."

"You mean that your being is attracted to its like kind or vibration?"

"Exactly. A sorcerer who thinks so much of events, manipulating others, broken promises, anger, fear, hate, and jealousy will be drawn to the lowest levels of spirit after death."

"In this life too, I should imagine."

"Oh, yes, that is for sure. But on the other side it is much worse."

"Why is that?"

"Because you don't have the earth plain, the house of mirrors. The physical body that allows a person to move around and create has been discarded. You are left with soul vibrations that have been created through your experiences on earth."

"Can't you move out of that dimension with your intent?"

"No, and that's worse. You stay in that low, ugly slime for thousands of years."

"It must be awful."

"Yes, you stay in that dark, painful place for eons of time, completely surrounded by the manipulations, anger, hatred, and pain that you've indulged in on earth."

"So the physical body provides a chance to change your karma?"

"Yes. That's really the sole reason for life in this schoolhouse." Agnes patted the earth and ran her fingers over some brown pebbles.

"Agnes, I've really got to talk about this fear inside of me. I can't live with all these awful images."

"What images are you talking about?" Agnes asked me as she squirmed around to get more comfortable.

"I told you about going into Bina's hut. She said that she saw terrible things around me. She asked me if I had had a misunderstanding with someone; if I had an enemy. I immediately thought of Red Dog, of course, and she said that he was doing me great harm. Then she asked how I felt physically, and after thinking about it, I realized I was feeling terrible. Even though Ani dragged me out of there kicking and screaming, I wanted Bina to help me. Maybe I'm going to die." I was close to tears.

"We're all going to die," Agnes answered, examining a tiny blue flower.

"Oh, thanks a lot. That helps. Agnes, I'm afraid. I see all these awful images of Red Dog coming at me and sending me evil."

"What kind of evil do you think he's sending you?"

"I don't know, but I'm sure it's terrible. I can't close my eyes without seeing his ugliness."

"That sounds pretty bad, Little Wolf."

"It is. I'm terrified and I don't know what to do."

"Are you sure it's Red Dog who is stalking you?"

"Oh, yes, I'm sure."

"How can you be so positive?" Agnes was now frowning at me.

"Because—because I see his face and I feel his energy tormenting me. Agnes, it's horrible. You got me into this mess and you've got to help me get out of it."

"So now it's me who got you into this mess?"

"Well, I'm your apprentice and you taught me how to regain the marriage basket." I knew I sounded like an hysterical child, but there was something about being on a windswept hill between Nepal and Tibet, so far from anything familiar. There was a primitive wildness in the air. I was feeling very frightened and was submerging completely into my little girl shield. What was worse, Agnes had thrown her head back and was laughing so hard that tears were running down her cheeks. Ruby was still peacefully sleeping.

"Agnes, what's so darn funny?"

"You are. You know so much and you know nothing."

"That's true. I'm very stupid." I wondered if my depression would ever hit bottom. Agnes sat up and stopped laughing. She just looked at me, shaking her head.

"How did you feel when you walked into Bina's hut?"

"I felt anticipation."

"I mean how did you feel physically?"

"I felt fine, maybe a little tired from all the traveling."

Agnes shook her head and started giggling to herself and muttered something.

"What did you say?" I asked.

Agnes looked at me almost sadly, then finally said, "What that sorceress Bina did was really dirty. I see why Ani was so angry with her. I would have been as well. That was really bad. She must be a very angry and unhappy woman."

Agnes looked off towards the mountains that were slowly being obscured by haze.

"Look at the magic dance of the Dorje Lapka, how she moves in and out of the clouds."

I too watched the Himalayas beginning to disappear from view as Agnes said something to herself in Cree.

"Why was she so bad?"

"Didn't Ani explain this to you?"

"I guess I didn't get it. I understand what she said, but I'm still afraid."

"That's why Bina is so bad." Agnes was looking very remote; her eyes were almost squinted shut.

"Agnes, please explain."

"There is negative phenomena in the world to some extent. You can send negative thoughts or energy. We all do that unwittingly when we're angry with someone or something like that. But I want you to understand, before we leave this hill, that negativity is never different from your own neurotic mind."

"What are you saying?"

"I'm saying that Bina is a sorceress, a black magician. She has tricked you."

"You mean that she was just fooling with me?"

"Yes, of course. You were fine when you walked in and you were not fine when you left. But she did nothing to you but perceive your own wilting psychic immunity. You were not holding your power, how could you, you gave it all to her. If she had said rupees are rice you would have believed her. She found the chink in your armor, so to speak."

"But it's true that Red Dog is after me, I feel it."

"You are a victim of your own imagination. In this case your imagination was unbalanced by Bina's tricky suggestion. She saw your fear and she used it against you. It's typical and not very clever, just ugly. She has helped you create a fear phenomenon that is neurotic. It's okay, it's a good lesson."

"I'm tired of lessons. I don't want any more. I want to go home. And I know Red Dog means to hurt me." I was crying and seeing awful images of him.

"I think Red Dog has other things to worry about. It's probably a bit warm where he is now," Ruby said as she rolled over and propped herself up on her elbows.

"What do you mean? How do you know where he is?" I wiped my eyes and glared at her.

"Haven't you heard? I thought you'd be the first to know," Ruby said, grinning at me.

"Heard what?"

"Red Dog is dead. He's been dead for two months."

"I don't believe you!" I almost yelled at her as I stood up.

"It's true," Agnes said.

"Why didn't you tell me?" I demanded of both of them.

"We knew you'd be so upset, we were trying to find the right moment," Ruby answered.

I paced around the top of the hill and finally sat down in front of Agnes.

"You're not kidding me, this is across the pipe, no joking around?"

"No joking. There are probably many people called Red Dog, but the sorcerer you knew is dead and Ben and Drum have completely disappeared. No one knows if they're dead or alive."

"What happened to him?"

"Nobody knows that either. Some men found him dead in his cabin. That's all we know." Agnes watched me.

"So this thing with Bina was a dirty trick. What a creep. She really scared me. My God . . ." I stopped talking. I picked up a stone and tossed it out toward the valley.

"Agnes, I don't know why you didn't tell me about this. How could you have let me suffer all this time? I've been agonizing over Red Dog and what he might be doing to me. I don't care what kind of lessons you want me to learn. I think this is incredibly unfair. In fact, I think I am going to just leave and go home. I don't think that I can work with you any more. I think that it was a very unkind trick to have played on me."

Agnes and Ruby sat on their stones looking at me almost as if they had not heard me. I put on my parka, turned, and walked down the trail. I looked across toward the Annapurna Himal, which were now totally obscured in mist. I felt that my own life, everything that I had tried to do, all my endeavors, all the books I had written had been for nothing. Somehow I felt as if a fog had come over my life too, and obscured all of my good feelings about what I had been doing. I thought back to something Agnes had said years ago about the fact that a warrioress needs a good enemy, and in a way I felt a loss for that enemy. It was a very strange experience. It was almost as if I hadn't wanted Red Dog to die. As I walked I kicked the stones in front of me and stubbed my toe. I sat down on a little grassy patch on a ledge looking down over the valley below. As I sat there moving in and out of feelings of depression, a new feeling of exaltation, excitement, and then peace began to overtake me. I began to realize that there had been an emptiness inside of me that my combat with Red Dog had created all these years, a feeling of tension and pain that I hadn't even been aware of. Now that the antagonism was gone from my life, I felt like someone who had just gotten out of an alcoholic marriage, someone who had escaped a person who had beaten them every day. I suddenly realized that that opponent, that deadly opponent, was out of my life. Red Dog had gone on to other levels, to other battles that had nothing to do with me. I had in some way been hanging on to the pain he had created. Bad habits can become like old friends and at first, when we lose them, we become angry. I realized even more deeply that as human beings, we don't like to lose anything, even something that is uncomfortable and causes us to lose sleep and be in agony. It is very strange how we are conditioned to accept a relationship, a situation that causes us so much difficulty. I remembered that Agnes at one time had said that women are like sponges. You can squeeze them until there is nothing left of them, squeeze all of the life out of them, the water, and let go of the sponge, the woman, and she goes right back to her original shape to go on with life. A woman has extraordinary endurance. There is a special power within a woman because she understands the true energy on mother earth. There is indeed a reason why mother earth has been called female. I started to cry as I looked out across the valley. Tears of relief, of joy; a great gift had been given me. I began to understand through this journey in Nepal about a darkness in my own soul that Red Dog had created. There was a place that I had allowed him to live within me, and I realized that there was actually a place within me that had needed that difficulty. I had had so much chaos in my relationship with my father as a child. I had experienced tension and pain all my life. It was what was familiar. Even though it was dreadfully uncomfortable it was known and it was all I knew of love. Somehow in a distorted and strange way, Red Dog had given me that same old familiar feeling of dread, terror, and unhappiness that I had lived with earlier. I remember one time that Agnes had me write down the feelings that I had as a child, the feelings that I grew up with in my home. Then she asked me, "How many of these feelings do you re-create in your daily life now that you're an adult?" I realized that the life situations were very different. I certainly wasn't married to a man like my father, but the stress I was under, the relationships that I chose, mostly romantic relationships, all gave me the same kind of stress and difficulty I had had as a kid. I began to realize the immense importance of giving that up. Agnes had looked at me at that time and said, "Lynn, now you know the reason you are on this good mother earth. Now you know why you chose the parents that you chose. You chose them to give you the problems or gifts that you have in this lifetime. They gave you a set of emotional problems that you need to solve and to understand. As a result of that, you will become much closer to being an enlightened woman. When you can live in happiness and joy and peace instead of tension and chaos and pain and terror, when you can chose happiness, the other side of the abyss from where you stood while growing up, you will be an evolved being. You will have done the work you have come into this lifetime to do."

As I remembered this conversation which had taken place so very long ago, I realized that I had come to a turning point, a closure in a sense, that the end of Red Dog marked the end of a period of my life. I realized with stunned surprise that my meeting with Bina had created a circumstance that had brought all of this to a head. Suddenly I saw clearly what an extraordinary manipulation sorcery and certain aspects of power can be. I thought about so many people in my life who tricked me into giving away my power, because I thought they were better than I. I always thought that they had more power. Certainly many of the relationships in my life were romantic ones that tended to take my power, not because the man actually took it, but because I was willing to give it. I chose people who would take it. I realized, now, that my relationships would be very different. Everything was going to change as I knew it. I understood why Agnes and Ruby had not told me before this time. I looked across at the Annapurna Himal as the slanting rays of sunlight from the sun hanging low in in the sky striated the clouds with pink and gold and fringes of orange. A lone hawk called its hunting cry as it swept high into the mountain air and swooped down again into the valley, the edges of his wings transparent with golden light. I looked back up the mountain, expecting Agnes and Ruby to be descending the trail, as they knew it would soon be getting very cold. But Agnes and Ruby were nowhere to be seen. I decided that I would go back up to the top of the hill where we had been sitting in hopes that they hadn't gone down another path. I realized that I owed them an apology. I wrapped my parka around my neck and closed the zipper as I started back up the mountain. Pieces of gravel were slipping under my feet as I walked quickly with excitement. When I got to the top of the trail, Agnes and Ruby were sitting just as I had left them. Their eyes were closed. They were in meditation, their faces bathed in red-orange sunlight. I sat down, not disturbing them. Pretty soon Agnes and Ruby both opened their eyes. Agnes looked at me and she scanned my face and began to smile. She put her arms around me.

"Agnes," I said, "I'm so sorry. I'm sorry for again not being worthy of you and for not trusting you and your decisions about what my teachings should be."

Agnes looked at me for a long time and she said, "My daughter, these lessons are not easy ones. Tell me what it is that you have learned."

I looked at her with a big smile. "I realize that I have come to a turning point in my life. There is no question that I made a place inside of myself for Red Dog to live, just like I made a place inside of myself for the marriage basket. I understand that in a sense I kept him alive, and that through my fear and my terror he lived off my energy. As I began to pull away from him I understand that he began to diminish. And I understand that in all relationships between men and women, between all of us, that this is a dynamic that occurs when we don't understand our own individuality, if we don't trust our own identity in the world. If my identity would fringe off into yours and yours into mine, we would be in what we call a co-dependent relationship. That's when we lose our ability to fulfill our dreams in this earth walk. That is when we become ill and weak and we give away our power."

Ruby snickered and shrugged her shoulders. "Well, Little Wolf, it's about time. You sure need a lot of dramas.

I looked at Ruby and laughed with her and said nothing.

Agnes was looking down the valley at the setting sun. "That's not really it, is it?" I asked Agnes and Ruby.

"Not it?" Agnes questioned.

"No. I did a lot of this agony to myself. Agnes, you were right."

"That's what I've been trying to tell you."

"It really was completely my imagination." I lay down on the ground and breathed freely for the first time in days. "Good grief, I wanted Bina to do a ceremony. She would have sacrificed some poor chicken over my head, and all for what? This is so sick, I don't want to discuss it anymore!"

"Thank the Great Spirit, it's about time," Ruby announced, getting up and brushing off her skirt with her hands. We walked arm in arm down the path picking wildflowers here and there for Didi and Ani.

It took me several days to fully digest this news. Red Dog had always been lurking in the shadows of my life, tearing away at my womanhood, my self-esteem, and my sense of peace. Even though he had caused me such pain, I was still saddened by the fact that he had died in such an extraordinary state of ignorance.

There is no demise
for thinkers of the mountains
thinkers of the sunrise.

—John Joseph Crimmins

CHAPTER TWENTY

A GATHERING
OF THE CLAN

I had walked down through the adobe and rock houses of the village to the big rock formations by the river. I sat on a rounded stone near the place where Bahni had been offered up to the Gods. I meditated there for a long while. A gentle warm breeze came up from the west, carrying the scent of terraced wheatfields from far across the valley. The whole event of her death and dismemberment had marked my trail in an important way. Any lingering sense or belief in superstition had been eradicated. Symbolically, the cutting apart of what had been Bahni's body also severed me from my attachment to maya and the illusions of physical life. Somehow Bahni's death and ritual had made me face my own mortality and forced me to explore my understanding of good and evil. The dark jhagrini Bina had made me confront my own illusions of right and wrong, but the contemplation that had gone on in my own heart after Bahni's death was what made me fully understand that there is no absolute good and no absolute evil. Ruby was correct. I was experiencing a sense of relief, as if the demons had fled.

The demons being the negativity of my own mind. I had cleared away a home within my soul for Windhorse to live. In my dreams I often went to the valley and visited with him in his small rock house. The comfort and peace that I was feeling was a new experience. Ruby was correct again; it was a good marriage. I talked to Windhorse about everything. He was delighted when I spoke of Suku and the people of Chepang and their clothes of jute and leaves. When I was troubled, he comforted me. When I was joyous, he shared in my joy. As I thought over my experiences in Nepal, I felt full, as if my journey here was nearing the end. I rose from the stone that had turned warm from the sun. I gathered wildflowers as I walked back to Ani's house. I was thinking about dinner and what I could prepare as a farewell feast.

But, as I neared the house, I was aware of an unusual silence. Where was Didi, who at this time of day was usually sitting on the portal talking to Ruby or Agnes and preparing tea? The front door that was open all day was now closed. I suddenly panicked. I pushed against the blue door and at first I thought it was locked because it wouldn't budge. I shoved it hard with my shoulder and it burst open. There was no one in the cooking room. I swept aside the curtain hanging in the doorway to the main room. The windows were closed. The cotton sleeping mats were rolled up neatly against the walls.

"Hello—namaste," I called out, but no one answered. Then I noticed that Agnes, Ruby, and Ani's packs were missing. I ran back into the kitchen and there I saw a note on the table. It was secured to the smooth wooden surface by a ritual purba carved out of wood in the image of Kali. My heart was pounding as I picked up the dagger in one hand and the note with the other. "Spirit Woman," the note began, using my medicine name, which Agnes and the others never used except in ceremony or at very serious times.

"When you hold the sacred purba in your left hand and this note in your right hand, be aware that the gathering of the clan has begun. It is time, Granddaughter. The signs are clear for your coming. Walk in balance. We wait for you until sundown. Bring your pack and medicine bundle. In Spirit, Agnes."

"Oh, great!" I yelled, looking at the purba in my left hand and the note in my right. "What does she mean by 'the gathering of the clan'? Oh, my lord, she must mean the Sisterhood. Here in the Himalayas? Why didn't they tell me?" I fled from one room to the other gathering my few things and putting them in my pack. I was in a complete tizzy. I was excited and scared.

"What signs are right? What does she mean, and how do I find them?" I yelled at the adobe walls of the house. As I zipped my blue pack closed, I noticed Agnes' eagle feather laying conspicuously on the yellow windowsill.

"She took everything, why didn't she take her favorite eagle feather?" I asked myself, picking it up and finding a long red thread attached to the quill. Then I remembered a trick she had taught me once in Manitoba. As she had instructed me then in her cabin, I tied the eagle feather, letting it hang from the three-foot length of the thread, from the center of the doorway. Then I sat down on the floor and closed my eyes. With all my power, I asked the eagle feather in which direction the women had gone. I knew to keep my eyes closed until the noise of hysteria had quieted in my mind. Finally, when I had reached the shaman's still point, I opened my eyes. Agnes' eagle feather was making a wide swing from center position to the north and back to center. I stared at it, a thrill running up my spine.

"They've gone up the Namtang Trail to the north," I said to the feather, holding it momentarily to my heart. Then I carefully wrapped it in red material and placed it in my pack to return to Agnes. I breathed deeply to stay centered. It was very clear to me as I ran down the trail from the house that I was being tested. I was being tested by power and the Sisterhood. I knew that the Sisterhood met every fifty years in a valley in the Himalayas. Where, I had never been told. Agnes, in a ceremony with Jaguar Woman and myself long ago in the Yucatán, had explained about this meeting, that it marked one of the big initiations of the clan. How could I have been so stupid as to have thought about going home and making a farewell feast?

I skirted the village, crossed the river on a narrow suspension bridge that stretched between two craggy granite cliffs and headed up toward Dorje Lapka. The Himalayas glistened white and pure like tall spires on the castles of the Gods. I noted the lowering position of the sun and broke into a run. I knew that if I did not reach Agnes by sundown I would have failed the first test and all would be lost. The thin air and increasing steepness of the trail caused me to to stop and rest often. I was furious with myself for having not done more exercise the past few days. I had been so exhausted that I had done virtually nothing but write about my experiences in Chepang and eat rice and biscuits. As I rounded a sharp curve in the path, I saw up ahead a Himalayan pine tree clinging to a shale-filled crevice on the side of the mountain. As I came to it, I untied Ruby's red silk scarf, which hung like a prayer flag from a low-slung branch. I breathed a sigh of relief, knowing I was on the correct path. I took a swig of water from my canteen and began with renewed strength to jog up the trail. But I could only run for ten minutes or so at a stretch, because the trail had become too steep.

I sat down on a low granite ledge to catch my breath and looked up to see the position of the sun. It hung in the sky, a golden orange ball, barely above the horizon line. Long, deep purple shadows traced across the trail from the tall Himalayan cedars that occasionally dotted the mountainside. I leapt to my feet and pushed myself into an uphill jog. My muscles were burning. I was alarmed that I had not yet reached Agnes. I knew that I had only minutes left to find her. Perhaps I was on the wrong trail, but I kept going. I was constantly aware of the ceaseless march of the clouds above me as I would run from one patch of shadows into a pool of sunlight and back into shadow. The play of light had an odd effect on me. I was slightly disoriented. I was running east with the setting sun at my back. Then the trail began to bend around an outcropping of granite boulders until I was actually running into the west with the setting sun blazing into my eyes. Just as I began to panic, running at my limit, I saw four figures ahead of me on the trail standing silhouetted against the flaming orange horizon. They stood still as if sentinels at a gateway. I stopped in my tracks, holding my hand up to shade the sun. For a moment I wasn't sure it was Agnes. Then I heard Ruby's familiar voice echoing out through the mountain crags.

"What took you so long?" Ruby asked.

"You read the signs, my daughter. It is good. May I have my eagle feather?" Agnes said, holding out her hand as the sun slid down behind the foothills below the Ganesh Himal range and disappeared. I reached into my pack, took out the wrapped feather and the red silk scarf, and handed them to Agnes and Ruby. Agnes touched the bundle to her forehead and put it away with her things. Ruby tied the scarf around her neck.

"Quickly, Lynn, before dark we must change your clothes," Ani said, holding out a brown woolen shirt and a simple woven jacket made of goat's fur that was fairly light but very warm.

"Why?" I asked. "What's going on?"

"You will be disguised as a boy from the Nar Valley." As Ani said this, she and Didi began to rub a mixture of pungent-smelling herbs into my skin and hair. I was instantly dark-complexioned.

"Does this stuff wash off?" I questioned.

"Yes, with a little scrubbing," Ani answered.

A cold wind came up from the north as it became increasingly dark. I took off my blouse and then decided to wear it under the wool shirt, because the wool felt prickly and I would need the warmth.

"Where exactly are we going?" I was almost afraid to ask.

"We are trekking into Tibet for a gathering of the Sisterhood of the Shields," Agnes said as she wound two heavy pashmina scarves around my neck and pulled one over my head and now-darkened hair that was pulled back and tied out of sight under my jacket and scarves.

"The Sisterhood, all of us in the Himalayas!?" I sat down in the dirt to let the whole idea sink in, all forty-four of us converging in Tibet. A wave of excitement ran through my body.

I stared at the women's faces as they continued to prepare me to look like a boy. Then I realized that all of them were dressed like the women from the Nar Valley, high in the mountains. I remembered that Ani's family had brought her down into the lower foothills of Nepal when she was a young child. I could tell by their heavier clothing, brown and black wool, with a splash here and there of reds and blues woven into their blouses and belts, that we were headed for much colder weather. Fortunately, I had worn my black tennis shoes, so the long dark pants covered me and we shared a few biscuits and some goat cheese.

"We are heading toward the border into Tibet tonight," Ani said, taking a big bite of cheese.

"Tonight? But we'll freeze," I said, astonished.

"As you know the borders into Tibet are all closed by the Red Chinese. I know of an ancient trail through the rocks. I think we can slip through unnoticed. But if we come upon soldiers, your disguise will be the only thing that will ensure our safety."

"This is too dangerous, Ani. Why can't we just meet in Nepal?" I asked with renewed fear inching up my spine.

Agnes reached out with a gloved hand and held my arm. She looked into my eyes in the encroaching darkness. Her eyes flashed as if there were tiny shards of flint around her pupils.

"This is a very important gathering, my daughter. It happens only once every fifty years."

"You were all here fifty years ago? How could that be?" As a look of disdain crossed the women's faces, I realized how stupid my question was and went on. "Will we be gone a long time?"

"That depends on you, Little Wolf, so only the Great Spirit knows how many years it will take," Ruby said, getting herself more comfortable on a flat rock.

"What do you mean it's all up to me?" I looked at the women one by one.

Ani searched in her pack for something. Finally she found what she was looking for. She held in her hand the tiny soapstone horse with crystal eyes that I had carved for her so many months ago. Ani held it up to the flame from the small butter lamp. The crystal eyes sparkled and looked momentarily alive.

"Unknown to you, Lynn, this wild horse is the key. Long ago, our sisters, the power holders, lived in a high valley with their families. Entrusted to them were the ancient texts of wisdom. This wisdom has come down through the ages from the Star Sisters and has been protected by the Sisterhood in a different way," Ani said.

"What do you mean a different way?" I asked as the five of us huddled together for warmth.

"Because of the shift of energy forces on this mother earth about three thousand years ago, from a matriarchal world to a patriarchal one, some truths had to be hidden. The wise ones, women of the Sisterhood, memorized the knowledge and the teachings and handed it down orally from apprentice to apprentice. Around two thousand years ago, to disguise the valley and its sacred treasure all the women left. In their place a lineage of monks have maintained the halls of learning where the mysteries were taught. They are gentle and they know nothing of the history of the valley. All they were told was to guard the great text and never to enter the sacred room where it is kept."

"That's such a long time, Ani," I said.

"Yes. Fifty years ago we did ceremony in Tibet and expected to find the valley. But the last key was missing and we discovered that it was not yet time to re-enter the valley of Luktang. Now it is time, and I want you to realize the true workings of the Great Spirit within the mystery of what we call life. From across the seven seas, from a tiny cabin in the north of your country you, have managed to bring us the final missing link, the mustang."

"But what does a wild horse have to do with the valley of Luktang?"

"It is long and complicated, my child, and we must begin to move or we will be frozen to the trail. But I'll tell you, when you brought me your inspirational gift—I knew many things, it told me much. I knew then that your spirit husband would be Windhorse. He is of the Mustang clans and his valley is in those mountain ranges," Ani said, pulling her jacket around her shoulders.

"You mean there is a physical place where he lives?"

"Not exactly. For everything that is physical, there is a spirit counterpart. Therefore, for everything that exists in spirit there is a physical correspondence on the earth. His power area is mustang. That was the first thing. Then I realized that the way to Luktang had been obscured to us because we had forgotten something very important."

"What was that?"

"We had forgotten what I was just telling you."

"How do you mean?"

"We had forgotten that something cannot exist in only one reality. It must exist in all dimensions. If a path has been lost to you in the physical world, there is a reason. Usually it means a test. It means that you must stretch your abilities and begin to travel into other dimensions. The valley of Luktang is where the spirit is brought out of its prison of matter. We kept looking for a physical path that had been lost to us. We searched everywhere with no success. If Windhorse was your spirit husband-to-be, I knew that the horse carving was a deeper sign. There is an ancient trail into Tibet that goes along the lower edge of the Mustang district. It was known to my power holder. She took me there once long ago on a pilgrimage to a sacred mountain. She told me never to forget the way. There would be a time, she said, when I would return and the mountain would tell me what I needed to know. We will go there now. I am confident that this is the way," Ani said, standing up.

"But, Ani, can you be sure?" I asked.

"You brought me a tiny windhorse. It is a symbol on the prayer flags of Tibet for the pre-enlightenment state of buoyancy and joy. You must ride that windhorse into the plain of enlightenment. It is clear to me," Ani said as we set off by moonlight up the trail.

We followed Ani, and Didi walked last. I was not as sure as Ani of the signs, after all it was just a simple carving. As I walked, a sense of knowing began to well up inside my heart. For some inexplicable reason I knew that we were moving towards an extraordinary event. It was true, I thought. I saw Windhorse in my mind, shaking his head and laughing at my continual doubt. I knew it was all true, and that gave me renewed strength as the air became thinner and icy cold.

We walked all night. By morning we were exhausted, made a meager breakfast of tsampa and rice with tea. We said almost nothing as we curled up next to one another and slept a few hours. Ani woke us and we set out on a trail to the northwest. It was on this track that we passed into Chinese-occupied Tibet two days later. The journey was through exquisite country of green meadows dispersing into high shale deserts of gray and brown stone. Along the way, Ani and Didi would take a few moments to point out different healing herbs and plants. At one point, we had walked down into a small lush canyon and Ani had stopped before a smooth-barked tree. The tree had only three large branches at the top with three large green leaves.

"This is almost an exact replica," Ani said, "of a diagram my power holder drew me of a sanskrit Tree of Medicine. The branch to the left represents the left part of the human body, or the vayu. The vayu is aggravated by the suppression of natural urges, like fear, lack of sleep, grief, sexuality, or taking in food before your previous meal is digested." Ani stroked the trunk of the tree with care. Then she pointed to the center branch. "That branch is named pitta, representing the human trunk, and it becomes diseased by the intake of alcohol, too much sun or fear, sharp things, spices, and eating irregularly. The right branch represents the body's right half and is called the kapha. That half becomes ill from too many sweets, milk, meat, excessive cold food, and too much sleep during the day. Of course, Tibetan medicine is a lifelong study and I'm sure you'd find it very interesting," Ani said, pinching my dark-brown cheek.

"I wish we could talk about it more," I said as we continued to walk through the valley.

As we started up a steep trail on the other side, it was getting toward evening. The shadows on the surrounding mountains were becoming hard-edged and black. Ani and Didi stopped us for a few minutes and adjusted our clothes.

"The trail is narrow and steep ahead. Be careful, for we are now across the border. We are in Tibet," Ani said.

We continued to go slowly, watching the placement of each footstep. There was a fast-moving river plunging down the gorge leading to the valley hundreds of feet below us. I tried not to look down. As we struggled around a sharp corner of the path, it suddenly widened. Ani held up her arm for us to stop. Coming toward us were three Red Chinese soldiers in dark uniforms, carrying rifles. I immediately bent over and held my scarves over the lower part of my face. Agnes placed her arm over my shoulder as if to help me. The soldiers spoke loudly in Chinese for us to stop, pointing their rifles at our stomachs. Ani immediately began to speak to the heavy-set sergeant. There was a stream of Manang and Nepalese words and much gesturing on both their parts. Ani pointed at me and then placed her hands over her heart. Then she showed him the sma sarkara curna, a medicinal preparation supposedly for my ailing father. By the end of their long conversation, the sergeant took some of the concoction for his own sick father and with tears of gratitude allowed us to hurry on by as long as we promised to return within two weeks. All this time Ruby had been watching the other soldiers, who seemed terrified of her and appeared very glad to leave us behind as they left with their sergeant.

After they disappeared Ani explained that she had told

him we were from the Nar Valley and were healers returning home to help my father. Ani said that the sergeant had been in grief over his own father, who was dying of diabetes. We hugged each other and continued on until well after dark.

As the crescent moon began to climb in the navy blue sky, we reached a place in the trail where two high mountains nearly met at the base. This created a very narrow passage. As we walked we could almost touch both cliff sides with our outstretched arms.

"Ani, could we stop for a while and eat some tsampa?" I asked just as a strange groaning sound was heard. The earth under our feet began to tremble and Ani yelled.

"Hug the cliff walls," she said, as she curled up in a ball against the mountain.

We all did the same as huge boulders and shale pounded into a large pile in front of us. When the thunder of the moving rocks subsided, we uncurled and stood up.

"The trail is impassable," I said, looking up at the huge vertical boulders blocking our way. "What can we do now?" I asked, brushing small stones and dust out of my clothes.

Ani sat down on a rock and said nothing for several minutes. Then looking around at me, she said, "The mountain has given us an avalanche. Let's eat something and then I'll tell you what I think."

She's like silver, there's
silver clinging to her wrists,
to her waist. Her eyes are
like silver, light flattens
in them. The wind in the trees outside
is like silver. And in her dream
there is a man, and the color red,
and a horse laden with silver.

—David Rollison

CHAPTER TWENTY-ONE

POWER ON THE MOUNTAIN

Ani looked at me with power and tenderness in her eyes.

"The spirits of the mountain have presented you with a test. Power is located in your will," she said, placing her flattened hand on my solar plexus. "Creative acts manifest through the use of will. Pure will is what is bringing about the change," Ani said, taking pieces of pine branches that she had gathered and twisted together.

"What do you mean 'the change'?"

"The process that we call life is going through a great shift. We experience that shift in terms of energy. Energy is building now in all of its forms."

"Why is that?" I asked, pulling my white pashmina shawl close around my shoulders.

Ani looked toward the huge barrier of shale and rock that blocked the trail. "I perceive the past as being an enormous womb, a womb of many births. But the womb has been barren for a long time. We have experiences, in the past hundreds of years, the darkness of a womb without life, because only balance can produce life," Ani said, gathering more pine branches and breaking them into pieces.

"But you say that there is a change?"

"Yes, my daughter, and change always brings difficulty to those who initiate something new." Ani sighed deeply as the light of the moon illuminated the deep crevices that furrowed her tanned cheeks. For a moment Ani's round silver earrings reflected an intense glow of white light, as if the moon had slid down to earth and hung momentarily from her ear lobes. "That period of darkness is ending soon. A magical child of light is preparing to be born. All forms of life, even if they are imbalanced and dark, fight to survive. That is why we feel resistance, but it has been written in the great books through the ages that the change is near. The womb is giving birth to the time of the child."

"Ani, what does that mean?"

"It means that we are all responsible for the reality and for all the reality that surrounds us."

"But what if you have nothing to do with a problem that happens to someone?"

"We make our own problems. They don't happen to us. If you are giving away your power or not you are still responsible." Ani was forming the pine branches into a circle like a large necklace.

"I don't understand."

"From now on, what anyone does on this earth is remembered. Now you will reap the effects of your acts. That is the meaning of the child. A long time ago this magical child had a name, but that's not important now. What matters is that people understand that the child is being born."

I looked around at Agnes, Ruby, and Didi, their faces almost obscured in the darkness. We all listened intently to Ani as she went on.

"A long time ago, the women called the great book in the valley of Luktang *The Child*."

"Why would they call a book of wisdom *The Child*?"

"Because the book contains the remembrances of ages past and the eons of time to come." Ani reached forward and poured some hot buttered tea into a cup and handed it to me. I sipped some, grateful for its warmth, and passed it to Ruby.

"You mean that this book contains a history of people?"

"It contains a history of higher thought and a history of thought to come."

"How can there be a history of something that has not yet happened?"

"The history is a remembrance of patterns. Truth is in the patterns and meanings, not the words or events that make up that meaning. In a sense, the next age is a reaping. The patterns are there and can be read. The child has been conceived and will be born. The star seeds have been planted and we are all responsible for their care. No longer can we hide behind the veils of ignorance. With the birth of the child, the veils of ignorance will be torn away." Ani held up the pine-branch necklace, looking for holes.

"I can't imagine a world without profound ignorance and resistance to change," I said as Ani lay down the branches and poured more tea.

"There is a chapter in the book that my power holder told me I must read one day before I pass on. She knew of your coming and she knew that the book would be restored to the Sisterhood."

"How did she know that?"

"Because it is time and it has been written in the caves of Chepang that during this period the way back to the valley would be found."

The ground was getting very hard, so I moved to be more comfortable.

"Are the caves anything like the one we were in with Suku?" I asked.

"Yes, near there. Suku and her people are guardians for them. The wise ones know of these caves and their prophecies. Suku asked what shape you had discovered when you entered her cave. The shape was a key for her. She also read your shadow as you entered. It was different from anyone's shadow who had been there before you. It has always been that way. So, you see, it has all been written by the Gods, and it is our job to understand." Ani pursed her lips as she looked at me.

"Does that mean we have no free will?" I asked.

The women burst into laughter.

"Why is that so funny?" I couldn't help but giggle at the way they were rolling around on the trail.

"Perhaps when you arrive in Laktang and open the book, it will all be revealed to you," Ani said as she got up holding several pine branches.

"Talk, talk, talk," Ruby said, elbowing me in the ribs and making me jump.

"How are we going to get past this avalanche?" I asked Ani.

"We will do a ceremony," she answered.

"How will a ceremony move all this rock?" I asked, feeling hopeless.

"That's for you to discover and we will follow. Remember, there are no accidents, and there is a reason for the mountain to test you in this way," Ani said as she began to prepare a circle of stones.

Didi piled wood scraps in the center for a small fire. Agnes and Ruby were laying out various bundles and smoothing the ground, as I did, with their hands. The moon was rising full above us. We all but ignored a cold wind that was coming down from the north, carrying the scent of pine trees high in the Himalayas. We worked fast, because it was cooling off so quickly.

Before long, we were seated in a circle. Ani passed me some water from her canteen and told me to drink. The fire, dancing on the trail, sent eerie reflections onto the gray slag cliffs that towered above us. It was as if the mountain spirits had come alive in fantastic huge forms and were performing an ancient ritual surrounding us. We all watched the undulating shadows for a moment. Then Ani and Didi placed the long pine-wreath necklace over my head. It hung loosely around my neck. It held the aroma of the north.

"We will begin. Take this wild horse that you carved for me. He represents buoyancy and joy, the state of mind just before enlightenment. Ride that state into another world. Show him to the doorkeeper and he will let you pass," Ani said as we began to chant a Nepali prayer that she had taught us. Our voices echoed softly between the canyon walls.

I put the horse in my breast pocket as I closed my eyes. I kept seeing a vision of Agnes and myself in the north of Canada. I kept trying to clear it away, because I thought I was losing my attention, but it was too vivid. Finally I relaxed and watched it. I was saying to Agnes in the vision:

"I can't Agnes. I just can't go on. This is too hard," I was crying.

"Why are you sad, my daughter?"

"Some of the native people don't understand what we are doing. They think I'm trying to hurt them, and I love them so much. They don't see the love I have for them or the reason I am writing."

"You write about the beauty of balance. I am Indian, but what I have taught you is about a universal truth not traditional Indian medicine. A truth that has no cultural boundaries. If I had been a Buddhist or of any other religion no one would have cared about our work together. I chose to come to you as an Indian because the native peoples of the world are first-born. The primal nature has never been integrated into the whole of consciousness and it must become so. That is one of the meanings of the sacred child. A rebirth must occur to accomplish this task. We must unite, all of us. That is the original message of the medicine wheel. The old ones had no hate; they could not conceive of jealousies or hurting anyone. They lived in a time of freedom. Now it is different and many have forgotten the old ways. I don't mean old ceremonies, I mean the old, gentle, wise path of the heart. I said long ago that native peoples stand in the place of the woman on mother earth. They are under siege, just like feminine consciousness. But native people, like woman, symbolically represent the regenerating principle of our mother the earth. They understand and should be the keepers of the primal power of this planet. Destruction of this power has become a cult of fascination for the whole world for many ages. Now destruction itself is being destroyed with the coming of the child. Those who choose not to see but to destroy will reap the effects of their acts and will also be destroyed. It is the law of the time. People today have to fight to live. But a true warrioress fights from the heart, and that is what is forgotten. But the heart will be remembered. You have taken nothing from anyone, not even me. You are simply remembering what you already knew."

"I understand, Agnes, but still I don't know if I can go on."

Agnes put her arm around my shoulder. I looked down at her hand and saw white feathers. I jumped back. Agnes had changed into a different being. She looked like a huge white archangel with a sword of fire in her right hand. I blinked my eyes. I couldn't believe what I was seeing. Actually she was not male or female. Her face was radiant and young and she smiled at me.

"The only truth you and all others must take into the new age is this: Know that you have prepared for a long time and that now all you must do is go on. That is your responsibility."

Silently and with a glow of intense white light the vision slowly faded. I found myself still sitting around the fire chanting and holding Agnes' hand. I spun my head to look at Agnes watching me.

Agnes winked at me as we went on with the ceremony.

Days are sieves to filter spirit,
reveal impurities, and too,
show the light of some who throw
their own shining into the universe.

—Rumi
Tr. by John Moyne and Coleman Barks

CHAPTER TWENTY-TWO

THE VALLEY OF LUKTANG

This was one of the first cere-
monies I had done where no dizziness or physical changes in
my body were occurring. In fact, my mind was feeling more
clear and perceptive than ever before. I sat with a blanket under
me and over my legs. I felt an unusual sense of warmth, with
not a trace of tension or discomfort anywhere in my limbs. I
followed my breathing for a while. Each breath was effortless
and the air felt pure. The women were chanting, but I was
chanting inside my head rather than saying the sounds. I felt
disconnected from everyone, which was unusual. Then I began
to feel a heaviness or pressure as if the pine wreath weighed
a hundred pounds and was pushing me back. Finally I quit
trying to bear the weight and I lay back on the ground. No one
seemed to mind, so I stayed there feeling very comfortable and
rather sleepy. I closed my eyes and enjoyed a deep sense of
strength and well-being. I was struggling, at the same time,
not to drift off into a deep sleep. After a while I heard the ruffle
of wings and a shadow crossed over the fire from the northwest.
No one else seemed to notice. I looked up to a rock above me
and to the left. Lurking there, with black wings shiny and
partially flexed, was the Nari. He was the Crow Eagle that had

accompanied me ever since my journeys into the sacred Dream-time of Australia. He had been with me for several years now, but did not often appear in this manner. Usually I would only see or sense his shadow. No one else sees him, but the women of power always sense his presence and nod with respect.

Nari, as I have come to call him, surprised me with his presence. I had not seen him during our journey in Nepal. He looked like a vulture as he watched me with his fine black head tilting toward the stars. He held something in his beak that was white like paper. As I looked at him, he lifted off of his granite platform and swooped silently down over my head, dropping the piece of paper in front of me. He flew off to a rock farther away. Still the women kept on chanting, as if they had not seen a thing. I picked up the paper and unfolded it.

"This ceremony is for you, Spirit Woman—as it is for all women. The soul of the mountain has sent you a gift. The gift lives beneath the avalanche of blockage that prevails within all sentient beings at this time. The mountain has sent you a sign. The trail is impassable and yet it must be followed. Your life has been thus. To reach the next level you must find the gate-way within your own being and the trail will become available to you once again. You wear the shield of trust and innocence on your chest. Follow the shield into your heart and be reborn. The Nari will lead you to Luktang."

I took a deep breath and relaxed my body, still holding the note in my left hand. I noticed that I was getting very warm. Ani and Didi had moved closer to me. I wore a deerskin med-icine bag around my neck with a South shield spiral design beaded on to one side. As I held the bag between my fingers, I felt something new and sharp inside. I wondered for a mo-ment what it could be, when all of a sudden, I had the sensation that the South shield spiral was whirling on the surface of my chest and then inside of me. It was as if I held the Grand Canyon, open and vulnerable within me. The spiral spun like a top, clearing me of any residual psychic debris and leaving me in the most extraordinary state of open-hearted love and trust. For a long time I stayed immersed in that state of joy. Then my body, even before I willed it, began to move. Not visibly on the outside surface, but on some inner cellular level. There was a sucking sensation, like the pressure from a whirl-pool throughout my body. As if I were folding my spirit hands together, I clasped them and dove into the sacred spiral whirling inside my chest. I was turning myself inside out.

A darkness settled around me as I heard the distinct sound of rocks moving against rocks. I felt extreme weight all around me. For a long time I rested, unable to move. Then my body began to turn to the right like a drill far beneath the surface of the earth. I realized that somehow I was experiencing what it would be like to be deep within my own primal self. It was as if I were hundreds of feet underground, rolling around boulders and piercing through subterranean ledges and cliffs. Deeper and deeper I went until I discovered a blue wooden gateway in a pile of rocks. For a moment I hesitated. Then I reached out and pushed the gateway open with all my strength. I saw a light above me in the distance. With my fingers clawing and gripping I swiveled my body up and out of the stony depths until the light was in front of me. Something was jumping up and down in front of the glow that I realized was actually the moon. Then I saw it was the Nari pulling something with his beak. As he jerked his head I felt a pull on my solar plexus. I realized he was yanking on my luminous fibers, as if he held my soul in his beak. I knew to follow him. I scrambled out of the rocks and to my astonishment I realized that I was on the other side of the avalanche. The Nari jumped up and down, urging me to hurry. I began to run down the trail underneath the Nari, who was flying in frantic circles. As I looked up ahead, I saw that the snow-covered mountains formed a definite triangular shape that actually shimmered with reflected light from the moon. I remembered that Ani and Didi had spoken one day about a map that Ani's power holder had given her in a dream. She had said something about a pyramid shape formed by the mountains. When I had asked her what it was, she said it was the location of "Old Tibet."

The trail was winding down more and was strewn with rock as if it had not been traveled in years. I carefully watched where I was going. The Nari was having trouble maintaining his wingspan between the narrow sheer cliffs on either side of me.

Before long we came to a widening in the path and it leveled out into a green meadow. Several rhododendron trees edged the trail. The grass felt cushiony and soft under my feet. I looked around at this extraordinary canyon-like valley. Sheer cliffs appeared to edge the entire circumference. It looked like the path I had just traversed was the only way in or out. The Nari was circling high above me. As I looked up at him, I caught a glint of light from the other end of the small valley. As I ran toward it, I realized with an overwhelming charge of joy that it was a stone monastery with a golden spire reflecting the moon. I turned around as I ran, trying to take in this fantastically beautiful and remote place. I knew that I had found Luktang.

Suddenly there was a soft vertical shadow to the left of me. But as I turned to look at it, I could have sworn I saw Agnes, but instead a star pine stood there swaying gently. Then another shadow crossed my peripheral vision and I thought I saw Ruby, but instead a Himalayan pine tree stood next to the path. All of a sudden one shadow after another crossed the trail and I was running through a forest of sal and pine trees. There were forty-three trees and I knew, as tears of excitement washed my cheeks, that the Sisterhood of the Shields had arrived. I ran, placing my hand on one tree trunk after another. I ran until I reached the steps of the monastery. I saw a candle burning in the window. I rang a small bell that hung by the large, heavy wooden door. I realized that carved into the front door was a figure of a wild horse exactly like the one I had sculpted out of soapstone for Ani. Slowly the door opened. I felt like I was standing inside of a fairytale. A very old Tibetan monk peered out at me. He gasped when he saw that there was really someone standing there. He pulled me inside by my sleeve. I was still dressed like a boy from the Nar Valley. We stood inside of a small stone room with a fireplace at one end. Books on shelves lined the walls. The monk's narrow bed was next to the fire. I sat down, thanking him. The old monk responded in a language I had never heard. He gave me a cup of tea from his teapot that had been sitting by an opened tablet that looked like wood prints in some form of Tibetan. The monk and I stared into each other's eyes for a long time. He was trying to read something in my face. He must have found something sad, or what he wanted, because tears welled up in his eyes and splashed down onto his maroon robes. I showed him the mustang I had given Ani. He touched it gently with his long knobby fingers, tracing every inch. He slapped his knees with his hands and smiled the kindest smile I think I'd ever seen. Then he took my hand and steered me into a hallway that led to a closed door at the end. As we stood in front of the doorway he reached around his neck and pulled out a key from under his shirt. Lifting it from around his neck, he handed it to me. I looked at him with surprise as he indicated the lock on the door. Then he handed me a lit candle and, sobbing into his sleeve, he returned to his room and gently shut the door. I looked at the key, which was very old and made of heavy iron. I wondered about the monk keeping something so large around his neck. It was about four inches wide with several angles forming the key. It looked like an abstract version of a Kachina doll from the Southwest.

Taking the key, I tested it in the lock and found that it couldn't be turned but was designed to slide sideways. There was resistance in the lock, as if it had not been used in a long time. Finally, after struggling for several minutes, there was a click. I gave the door a shove, but it didn't budge. I placed my shoulders against it and tried again. This time, in a cloud of dust, adobe chips, and cobwebs, the door opened. To my surprise, a candle was burning on a central table. Windhorse sat at one end and next to a huge book with an ornately carved wooden cover.

"Close the door. I am only here to help you and give you love." Windhorse smiled at me.

"But I thought no one had been here for a very long time," I said, so very happy to see him.

"No one has," he said, laughing at my astonishment. "Come. We have very little time." Windhorse motioned to a chair next to him.

As I sat down he put his arms around me and held me close. The journey into Luktang had exhausted me and I was having sensations of heat, dizziness, and lightheadedness. His embrace renewed my balance and strength. I looked into his dark eyes and knew that I had returned home; it was a land deep inside my own heart.

Next Windhorse took my hand and together we placed our open palms on the book called *The Sacred Child*. The cover of the book felt warm as if it were truly alive in some way. The carving was of trees and vines beautifully woven together. The cover was worn as if it had been well used. Together we began to turn the pages of the book. At first I was very disappointed, because the odd letters were unrecognizable to me. About half-way through, Windhorse took my fingers and placed them on the characters themselves. They were raised almost like braille.

"Close your eyes, my Spirit Wife," he said. "Let the child give you her message."

As soon as I closed my eyes I saw myself as a ball of intense light, as if I were watching from a corner of the room. Wind-horse also appeared to be a bright sphere of light floating over the table. For a long time we just floated like clouds in a trade wind, gently going up and down and around the room. I felt the urge of infinite, continuing life as we circulated around the open book. As we hovered over the table, I felt a pulsating sensation that became intense as our light touched and then merged together. Then our breathing stopped and our light dropped slowly down into the magical child. I felt a new throbbing, a new heartbeat; the heartbeat of what I can only call God. It was part of us and yet part of all Creation, but singular and within the profound silence of unceasing life. Then I heard an old female voice saying:

"A certain state of mind is needed to enter Luktang and to even find the entrance. The teachings here are for your higher self alone. The valley is like a temple. Your heat is the password of transformation and your body must be left at the entrance. The teachings give the soul rebirth and higher wisdom. Mother earth is the garden of the spirit. The spirit is planted here so that you may be born into a physical body. The valley is your home and your passageway out of the sacred dream called sentient life. As you turn each page I will give you a view of your life patterns."

Slowly a page turned and a vision of a grotesque being leapt out at me. It was frothing at the mouth and writhing in internal agonies. Instantly I saw all my fears manifested in this gargoyle of a creature. Then another monster and another began to surround me, tearing into my sphere of light with their talons. As each page turned there was a different monster with sounds of earth moving or water or fire rampant on a dry mountainside. The images described the emotions and karma of my lifetime.

There were also beautiful goddesses and peaceful moments within the flair of color and sound. The roaring sounds and clash of one monster then goddess, one upon the other, elicited one effect after another within me. As if the patterns of energy were burning up and down my being, disintegrating any psychic debris that was found.

"Life is a planting of the spirit so that a body can be formed from the dying seed. The monsters you have seen are the bardos, or stages of life, that you have lived on this earth. Without this earth, the seeds of the spirit would have no place to be born. You are a keeper of this mother garden. The Luktang Valley has been found again. The wisdom will remain safe here. You may return at will. That is the meaning of your journey here."

Our spheres of light were faltering and becoming dim. I was becoming very uncomfortable. Seeing this, Windhorse pushed up against me. I experienced a shove and a loud whooshing sound as the balls of light dissipated.

Windhorse and I closed the book. Again we stood in our forms looking at each other. He smiled at me as he backed away toward the corner of the room. A great heaviness suspended my body so that I could not move. I wanted to ask him so many things, but a fog enveloped the room. There was nothing but darkness, silence, and peace.

Death be not a hanged man
but a gracious teacher
remembering my name.

—John Joseph Crimmins

CHAPTER TWENTY-THREE

IT IS GOOD TO HAVE A DREAM

I felt the prickles of the pine wreath. The pine needles were poking through my shawl and jacket. I opened my eyes. I was still lying on the trail. The fire was out and Ani, Didi, and Agnes were sipping tea and looking at me. They were shaking their heads. The sun was an orange ball edging up over the mountain peaks.

"Well, lazy one, you missed it all. You slept through the whole experience," Ruby said, shaking her head and poking my shoulder.

"What do you mean?" I asked, holding my head because it was throbbing.

"We had to leave you here while we went into Luktang. It's a wonder some tiger didn't have you for dinner." Ruby was chuckling to herself.

Then I remembered the extraordinary dream I had just had. "It seemed so real. I saw Windhorse and the book," I announced, looking at Ani.

"Tell us what you saw, my daughter," Ani said.

I took a sip of tea and told them the whole story. Every once in a while Ruby would cluck her tongue and say something like, "I wish I could have dreams like that."

I couldn't believe it was all just a dream. When I was completely finished telling the story, Ani came over and sat across from me. She took my hands and held them to her heart after I gave her back the mustang carving. The carving was resting in her lap. Tears were in her eyes.

"Now you know the way into Luktang. The great *Book of the Child* will remain there for study. We will see you there often and share the wisdom. Your journey here is complete. Remember that the valley that is nowhere is your true home. It is good to have a dream," Ani said as she kissed my forehead and took the pine wreath from my neck.

For the last ten years, I've been describing my learning and my path. It has been a joy to do this. In continuing my journey, I would be grateful if you would share your insights with me.
Please write me at:

> *Lynn Andrews*
> *2934½ Beverly Glen Circle*
> *Box 378*
> *Los Angeles, CA 90077*

Please send me your name and address so I can share any new information with you.
In Spirit,